The Identity Crisis

Volume 1

By:

Pastor J. Henley

Scriptures are from the following Bible versions:
NLT, ASV, NIV, KJVA, ESV, and KJV.

Written by: Pastor J. Henley

Registered by the Library of Congress
ISBN: 979-8-234-07839-1
Printed in the USA
First edition 2026

Published by:
Blessed with Words Publishers
434.806.5357
Bwwordspub@gmail.com
Blessedwithwords.org

Table of Contents

Introduction

There is a quiet struggle that has persisted across every generation. This struggle does not always make headlines, yet its effects are visible in how we think, live, and perceive ourselves. We are constantly surrounded by voices—through culture, media, history, tradition, and power—each attempting to define who we are. Over time, however, the vision of Black and Brown people has often been distorted, replaced, and misinterpreted, leaving us with a profound identity crisis.

This book directly confronts that reality. Many Black and Brown individuals have inherited a false sense of identity without questioning its accuracy. We have embraced narratives whose origins we do not fully understand, living within systems that benefit from this confusion. When identity is unclear, purpose becomes uncertain. This book, therefore, is not merely about discovering who we are—it is about uncovering hidden truths and redefining our identity through the lens of biblical history and theology, world history, and black history. This book is designed to challenge readers to examine connections from new perspectives. For too long, we have trusted voices that have not always treated us fairly to define and teach our identity, while overlooking credible voices within our own ethnicity. It is my sincere prayer that, through this book, you will take the time to listen with an open heart and mind.

Truth has a way of disrupting what is familiar before it establishes what is real. Let me be clear: I am not anti-Semitic, for that would mean opposing my own people and ancestors. Likewise, this book does not promote racist ideas. Racism involves power and is typically directed toward those who are marginalized or classified as minorities. My purpose is to encourage deeper reflection, challenge you to question assumptions, and help you see beyond surface-level understandings. This work is more than information—it is a transformation. When identity is restored, clarity follows; when clarity is achieved, purpose ignites with power. Therefore, it is imperative that we understand who we truly are—and the first step is to come to terms with the Bible's reliability and significance.

CHAPTER ONE

I Believe the Bible!

First things first, I believe the Bible is the inspired Word of God. I believe it reveals the character of God, recounts what He has done, and instructs us on how to live in response. From Genesis to Revelation, it tells a unified story of redemption, truth, and hope—one that transcends time and culture. Because of that, our faith should not rest on shifting opinions or cultural trends, but on the eternal foundation of God's Word. In a world of ever-changing values, the Bible stands as our unshakable guide and recorded account of HIStory.

Faith is essential to believing in the Bible.

> *"Faith is the confidence that what we hope for will actually happen; it gives us assurance about things we cannot see" (Hebrews 11:1, NLT).*

Faith is what allows us to embrace the Bible's spiritual truths—many of which go beyond human logic or physical evidence. Scripture not only presents historical accounts or moral teachings; it also makes claims about the nature of God, miracles, and eternal life, realities that require trust in what is unseen. Without faith, such claims might seem far-fetched or merely symbolic. But faith bridges the gap between what we can comprehend and what God has revealed. It opens the door to a personal relationship with God that is built on trust, intimacy, and belief in His promises.

Whether we believe in God or not, we exercise faith every day to some degree. We believe that the sun will rise in the morning, that the floor beneath us will hold our weight, that the food we eat won't harm us, and that the people we love will still be there tomorrow. We get into cars believing we will arrive at our destination safely. We lie down at night believing we will wake up in the morning. Much of life operates on unseen trust because faith is woven into the fabric of everyday living. Even the skeptic exercises faith. A person may reject God because they trust only what can be proven, yet they still rely daily on countless things they have never personally verified. The real question is not whether a person has faith, but where that faith is placed.

The Apostle Paul affirms in 2 Timothy 3:16–17 that "*All Scripture is inspired by God.*" The term "inspired" (Greek: theopneustos) means "God-breathed," indicating divine origin through human authorship.[1] The Bible forms the foundation for Christian doctrine. It reveals who God is, who we are, the way to salvation, and how we are to live in holiness. But is it legitimate? Christ Himself faced that question. People wondered if His teachings were truly divine. He answered, "*My teaching is not mine, but of him who sent me. If anyone is willing to do His will, he will know of the teaching, whether it is of God or whether I speak from myself*" *(John 7:16–17, KJV)*. In the same way, those who align themselves with God will be able to discern that the Bible is indeed His Word written by mankind, for mankind.

---

[1] 2 Timothy 3:16–17 (NLT). The Greek word theopneustos, translated "inspired," literally means "God-breathed," signifying that the Scriptures originate from God Himself. See Wayne Grudem, Systematic Theology (Grand Rapids: Zondervan, 1994), 73–75.

Here's what's fascinating about the Bible: it is composed of individual books, written by different authors, across various time periods, and from diverse perspectives. And yet, there is a remarkable cohesion throughout the Scriptures. From Genesis to Revelation, the Bible unfolds a unified narrative centered on God's redemptive plan. Even though it was written over centuries by diverse authors, it remains consistent in its themes and harmonious in its ultimate message: the story of Christ. The book of Genesis introduces both the problem and the promise. It sets the stage for what is to come, laying the foundation of humanity's need for redemption and God's intention to provide it. The remainder of the Old Testament builds on this promise, developing anticipation through a series of prophecies, covenants, and historical accounts that all point forward to a coming Savior.

Then, in the New Testament, we see the fulfillment of that promise through the life, death, and resurrection of Christ. His ministry and sacrifice bring clarity to Old Testament foreshadowing and reveal the depth of God's plan for salvation. Finally, the book of Revelation presents the culmination of this divine story—declaring the ultimate defeat of evil, the restoration of a chosen people, the unification of Christ and His Church, and the eternal reign of the Kingdom of God. When we gain a deeper understanding of the Bible, we begin to see Christ revealed throughout every book—woven into its writings, themes, and messages. Even though the name of Yahshua the Messiah may not be explicitly mentioned in each book, the stories, symbols, and characters consistently foreshadow or point to the person and redemptive work of Christ. Scholars widely recognize this coherence as a defining feature of the Bible.[2]

The Bible is widely recognized as a collection of 66 books in the Protestant canon, written over approximately 1,500 years by more than 40 authors from diverse backgrounds, including kings, prophets, and religious leaders.[3] This number does not include the more than 54 Apocryphal books, writings, and other fragments discovered over the centuries. The Old Testament was primarily written in Hebrew (with some Aramaic). In contrast, the New Testament was written in Koine Greek, reflecting the linguistic environment of the eastern Mediterranean during the first century.

The King James Version (KJV) should not be viewed as the original biblical text, but rather as an English translation produced in 1611 from the manuscript evidence available to scholars at the time. The New Testament used by the translators relied largely on the *Textus Receptus*, a Greek compilation based primarily on later Byzantine manuscripts, many of which were copied centuries after the apostles' original writings.[4] As a result, the translators worked from texts that had already undergone lengthy periods of manual transmission.

---

[2] See Luke 24:27; John 5:39. Many Christian scholars and theologians have noted that the Hebrew Scriptures contain typological patterns, prophetic themes, and symbolic imagery that point toward the Messiah and His redemptive work. See also Augustine, *Questions on the Heptateuch* 2.73; Leonhard Goppelt, *Typos: The Typological Interpretation of the Old Testament in the New* (Grand Rapids: Eerdmans, 1982), 17–35.

[3] The Protestant canon consists of 39 Old Testament books and 27 New Testament books, for a total of 66. The broader Christian tradition, including Roman Catholic and Eastern Orthodox communions, includes additional texts. See F. F. Bruce, The Canon of Scripture (Downers Grove, IL: InterVarsity Press, 1988).

[4] Bruce M. Metzger and Bart D. Ehrman, The Text of the New Testament: Its Transmission, Corruption, and Restoration, 4th ed. (New York: Oxford University Press, 2005), 152–153.

Because ancient manuscripts were copied by hand, textual variations naturally emerged over time. These differences were not always the result of intentional alteration; many arose from ordinary scribal activity, such as spelling inconsistencies, omitted words, explanatory additions, harmonization between passages, or copying errors.[5] This reality is common within ancient literature and is one of the primary reasons textual criticism developed as a field of study.

By the 18th and 19th centuries, scholars began uncovering manuscripts far older than those available to the translators of the KJV. One of the most well-known discoveries was Codex Sinaiticus, brought to scholarly attention by Constantin von Tischendorf in the mid-1800s.[6] Other important witnesses, including Codex Vaticanus and additional Alexandrian manuscripts, provided textual evidence dating much closer to the earliest centuries of Christianity.[7] These discoveries offered scholars earlier sources for evaluating the wording of the New Testament.

When researchers compared these earlier manuscripts with the later Byzantine texts underlying the KJV, they found numerous textual differences, including grammar, spelling, and word order. However, none of these necessarily undermined the credibility of Scripture, nor did they diminish the historical importance of the King James Version itself. The KJV remains one of the most influential English translations ever produced, shaping theology, literature, preaching,

---

[5] Kurt Aland and Barbara Aland, *The Text of the New Testament: An Introduction to the Critical Editions and to the Theory and Practice of Modern Textual Criticism*, 2nd ed. (Grand Rapids: Eerdmans, 1989), 280–281.
[6] David C. Parker, *Codex Sinaiticus: The Story of the World's Oldest Bible* (Peabody, MA: Hendrickson Publishers, 2010), 1–12.
[7] Bruce M. Metzger, *The Bible in Translation: Ancient and English Versions* (Grand Rapids: Baker Academic, 2001), 126–128.

and culture for centuries. At the same time, manuscript discoveries demonstrate that the biblical text has been preserved through a historical process involving copying, comparison, preservation, and scholarly examination.

For this reason, textual critics generally place greater weight on manuscripts that are closer in date to the original writings, since they are viewed as potentially preserving earlier readings. Consequently, many modern Bible translations draw on a wider manuscript base than the translators of 1611 did.

Some believers hold the view that the King James Version represents a flawless and final English form of Scripture. Yet the manuscript evidence indicates that the KJV itself was produced from later textual traditions and predates the discovery of several earlier manuscripts now considered valuable to New Testament scholarship.[8] After examining the manuscript tradition, historical evidence, and scholarly debates surrounding textual criticism, many conclude that the King James Version is a valuable and respected translation, but not the original or dcfinitivc form of the biblical text. From that perspective, honoring Scripture involves a willingness to examine the evidence carefully and thoughtfully, recognizing that these manuscripts have survived for centuries of transmission across numerous cultures, languages, and empires.

The term "Apocrypha" derives from the Greek word meaning "hidden" or "secret."[9] Many Protestants rejected these books from the

---

[8] James R. White, *The King James Only Controversy: Can You Trust Modern Translations?* rev. ed. (Minneapolis: Bethany House, 2009), 89–115.

[9] The term "Apocrypha" derives from the Greek apokryphos, meaning "hidden" or "secret." These texts were excluded from the Protestant canon for various reasons,

biblical canon because they were viewed as inaccurate or lacking the same prophetic authority as the Old Testament. During the Protestant Reformation, reformers such as Martin Luther regarded the Apocrypha as useful for historical and moral instruction but not as divinely inspired Scripture on a par with the Law, the Prophets, and the Writings.[10] As a result, these books were gradually removed from many Protestant Bibles. However, they remained part of the canon in the Catholic and Eastern Orthodox traditions, which continued to recognize them as sacred and authoritative.[11]

Many pastors will advise against studying the Apocryphal writings. However, I personally believe in the value of many of these texts and intend to reference some of them in this book. I believe several Apocryphal writings provide additional context and deeper detail that

---

including questions about authorship, historical reliability, and doctrinal consistency. See Bruce M. Metzger, An Introduction to the Apocrypha (New York: Oxford University Press, 1957).

[10] Martin Luther placed the Apocryphal books in a separate section of his 1534 German Bible, describing them as "books which are not held equal to the Holy Scriptures, and yet are useful and good to read." Many Protestant reformers questioned their canonical status because they were not part of the traditional Hebrew canon and were viewed as lacking the prophetic authority attributed to the books of the Old Testament. See F. F. Bruce, *The Canon of Scripture* (Downers Grove, IL: InterVarsity Press, 1988), 97–106; Martin Luther, Preface to the Apocrypha (1534 German Bible); Gleason L. Archer Jr., *A Survey of Old Testament Introduction* (Chicago: Moody Press, 1994), 66–68.

[11] Although the Apocrypha was included in many early Protestant Bibles (including the 1611 King James Version) it was typically placed in a separate section between the Old and New Testaments rather than among the canonical books. During the nineteenth century, the British and Foreign Bible Society's decision to cease funding the printing and distribution of Bibles containing the Apocrypha contributed significantly to its removal from many Protestant editions. Meanwhile, the Roman Catholic Church reaffirmed the canonical status of the Deuterocanonical books at the Council of Trent, and the Eastern Orthodox churches continued to recognize them as part of their biblical tradition. See F. F. Bruce, *The Canon of Scripture* (Downers Grove, IL: InterVarsity Press, 1988), 104–106; David Daniell, *The Bible in English: Its History and Influence* (New Haven: Yale University Press, 2003), 742–744; *The Canons and Decrees of the Council of Trent*, Fourth Session (1546).

can enhance our understanding of the Bible. That said, it is essential to research these additional manuscripts carefully to ensure they align with the truth of God's Word. At the same time, I recognize that many of these writings, whether biblical or Apocryphal, may have been tampered with or altered over the course of history. And this brings me to my next point.

Let me begin by saying this: history has been hijacked. Black history has been hijacked. The Bible and biblical history have been hijacked. And without question, religion has been hijacked. To hijack something means to unlawfully seize it and redirect it to a different destination or use it for one's own agenda. So, if history has been hijacked, what happens when that history is tainted, altered, or erased? The generations that follow become ignorant, and ignorance means "you don't know." This is why we must commit ourselves to studying, researching, and uncovering the truths that have been hidden, altered, or distorted over time, so that we can return to the truth as originally given. In doing so, we honor God's Word—not by mindlessly clinging to tradition, but by humbly and reverently seeking true understanding.

So, before we dive in, I want to begin by letting you know that I believe the so-called Black American is a descendant of the Hebrews in the Bible, and this book is intended to uncover that truth. The challenge with fully embracing this is that it has not been widely taught within the church. Many leaders are aware of this information, but the influence of white supremacy has conditioned them. Those who do know are often afraid of losing control and understand that illiteracy opens the door to manipulation.

Have you ever heard someone say, "I'm woke"? Why are people making that statement? I believe it's because people are starting to question what they have always been told. They are beginning to dig deeper and realize that there is more than meets the eye, and the truth is now being examined extensively. With the internet and technology at our fingertips, access to information is easier than ever. Previous generations did not have that kind of access. Some could not even read. Others had no internet and had to go to libraries just to read encyclopedias or look through historical books. Some were raised in strictly traditional environments, where thinking outside of what was passed down was uncommon. And while I believe that time is accelerating and knowledge is increasing, we, as people of color worldwide, are still not fully awake. This is much like Jairus's daughter in the Gospel of Mark, who was thought to be dead, but Christ declared that she was only sleeping.[12]

That's exactly where we are as a people. We are not dead—we are asleep. But the fact that you are reading this book is evidence that something is stirring. An awakening is happening, and before we begin uncovering the true identity of the Hebrews in the Bible, we have to take a serious look at what we believe about this topic. Did you know that the Bible is not just a spiritual text, but also a book of history?[13] In fact, it is one of the most important keys to understanding who we are as a people. One of the main reasons many people struggle to apply the Word of God to their lives, or why some

---

[12] Mark 5:35–41. Jesus told the mourners that Jairus's daughter was not dead but sleeping, then raised her with the words Talitha koum ("Little girl, I say to you, arise").

[13] The Historical Reliability of the Gospels by Craig Blomberg presents archaeological and historical support for the Bible's accounts of real people, places, events, and accurate history.

do not read it with conviction, is that they cannot see themselves in it. And when you do not understand identity, you cannot identify. Therefore, it is my sincere prayer that by the end of this book, you will gain a full understanding of who's who, because I truly believe that the key to navigating the end times lies in knowing who you are and knowing who others are in God's divine plan.

Reclaiming the Bible from Cultural Distortion

Let's begin by making another thing clear: The Bible is not a "White Man's Book." However, over time, it has been whitened in readers' minds. This distortion has occurred through the changing of names, the alteration of images, the way it was weaponized during slavery to condition the minds of the enslaved, the way it was used to conquer nations, and the way both science and recorded history, rooted in white supremacy, were manipulated to confuse and mislead readers. But to truly understand the Bible, there are a few essential truths you must know: The Bible is a book about the history of a specific people—a melanated people. We should never dismiss the Black presence in the Bible just because it does not use terminology coined through race, such as "African" or "Black." The people of the Bible were primarily people of color, living in regions where melanin-rich skin was a biological necessity due to the climate and geography.

The Bible is also both a prophetic and a literal book. Many understand the power this book holds, which is why its truth has so often been hidden, twisted, or suppressed. Originally, the Bible was written in multiple languages, and understanding those original languages (along with the meanings behind the words) greatly aids in proper translation and interpretation. Furthermore, the stories of the Bible were passed down through oral tradition—taught and preserved by word of mouth.[14] Entire communities depended on these teachings and the faithful recitation of Scripture to preserve the truth and pass it from generation to generation.

Many people recognize the power of the Bible, and the even greater power that comes when you understand the real truths contained within it. Did you know that the Vatican removed books from the Apocrypha, yet its version of the Bible still includes more than the standard sixty-six books found in most Protestant Bibles today?[15] This was not by accident. Because of the transformative power of true understanding, great efforts were made to maintain control over access to the Scriptures and to preserve institutional authority.

At the Council of Toulouse in 1229 AD, it was declared that laypeople were not permitted to possess copies of the Old or New Testament, nor any translations of those texts.[16] Later, at the Council of Tarragona in 1234 AD, it was ruled that no one could own the Bible in the Romance language. Anyone found in possession of such texts was required to turn them over to the local bishop within eight days of the decree or face consequences. The books were burned, and the

---

[14] Oral tradition was the primary means of preserving and transmitting Scripture in ancient Israel before texts were written down. See Susan Niditch, Oral World and Written Word: Ancient Israelite Literature (Louisville, KY: Westminster John Knox Press, 1996).

[15] The Roman Catholic canon includes 73 books, incorporating seven deuterocanonical texts (Tobit, Judith, Wisdom, Sirach, Baruch, and 1–2 Maccabees) not found in the Protestant Bible. See the decrees of the Council of Trent, Session IV (April 8, 1546).

[16] The Council of Toulouse (1229 AD) decreed: "We prohibit also that the laity should be permitted to have the books of the Old or New Testament." This was a local council convened by Bishop Folquet de Marselha to address the Albigensian heresy in southern France. See Censorship of the Bible, in New Catholic Encyclopedia, 2nd ed. (Washington, DC: Catholic University of America, 2003).

individuals, whether clergy or layperson, would be considered under suspicion until proven otherwise.[17]

One of the most well-known victims of this control was William Tyndale. He was labeled a heretic by the Roman Catholic Church for translating the Bible into English. In October 1536, he was executed by strangulation, and his body was then burned at the stake, all for his efforts to make the Bible accessible to everyday people.[18]

Another reason many do not truly understand the Bible is due to the various interpretations and translations that diverge from the original Hebrew and Greek texts. These differences can sometimes obscure or completely alter the intended meanings. To grasp the deeper truths of Scripture, it is necessary to study the original languages, consult tools such as Strong's Concordance and biblical dictionaries, and reference early texts, including the Hebrew Bible, the Apocrypha, the 1611 King James Version, and even older translations such as the Geneva Bible.

From roughly 500 AD to 1500 AD, the civilized world was dominated by the Roman Empire and its ecclesiastical heirs, which gradually co-opted the beliefs of the early Christian Church. They merged the teachings of Christ with elements of ancient Egyptian, Greco-Roman,

---

[17] The Council of Tarragona (1234 AD) ruled that no one could possess the books of the Old and New Testaments in the Romance language. Violators were required to surrender such texts within eight days. Voir D. Lortsch, Histoire de la Bible en France (Paris, 1910), 14.

[18] William Tyndale (c. 1494–1536) was an English biblical scholar who produced the first English translation of the New Testament drawn directly from Hebrew and Greek texts. He was convicted of heresy and executed by strangulation, after which his body was burned at the stake, at Vilvoorde near Brussels in October 1536. See David Daniell, William Tyndale: A Biography (New Haven: Yale University Press, 1994).

and Babylonian paganism. The pure doctrine that came directly from Christ and was faithfully recorded in the Bible posed a threat to the authority of the Roman Church. In response, the Roman religious system positioned itself as an intermediary between Christ and the believer. They taught that salvation could only be attained through the authority of priests, bishops, and cardinals. However, certain individuals rose in protest. The papacy responded with strict bans on translating or distributing the Bible to the general public. Only Jerome's Latin Vulgate was permitted, and only trained clergy were allowed to handle it. John Wycliffe secretly translated the Vulgate into English so the common people could understand it, and his translations were carefully copied and distributed despite strong opposition from the Roman Church.[19]

Roman authorities hunted down Wycliffe's followers, known as Lollards. These believers were tied to stakes, Bibles hung around their necks, and they were burned alive. Because Bibles were painstakingly copied by hand, every execution not only took a life but also destroyed an irreplaceable text. Forty years after Wycliffe's death, his bones were exhumed and burned by the Church of Rome in a symbolic act of condemnation. They carried out similar punishments on others, including Jerome of Prague, who was also burned for heresy.[20] This brutal opposition led to the Protestant Reformation. In 1408,

---

[19] John Wycliffe (c. 1330–1384) produced the first complete English translation of the Bible from the Latin Vulgate. His followers, known as Lollards, were severely persecuted. Forty-four years after his death, the Council of Constance ordered his bones exhumed and burned. See G. R. Evans, John Wyclif: Myth and Reality (Downers Grove, IL: InterVarsity Press, 2005).

[20] Jerome of Prague (c. 1379–1416) was a Czech theologian and follower of Jan Hus. He was condemned for heresy and burned at the stake at the Council of Constance in 1416. See Thomas A. Fudge, The Trial of Jan Hus (New York: Oxford University Press, 2013).

England made it illegal to translate or read the Bible in common English without a bishop's permission.[21] Yet despite these restrictions, the Bible continued to be translated and shared, eventually leading to the production of the King James Version.

Throughout these phases, much of the effort to restrict and alter Scripture was rooted in a desire to keep people from discovering their true identity—both the identity of the people in the Book and their identity within the Book. The Bible has been preserved, yes, but it has also been challenged, manipulated, and at times changed, all to suppress the truth of who God's people truly are. What, then, are some other reasons or challenges that people find difficult to reconcile with belief in the Bible?

Slavery: Trauma, Memory, and Misunderstanding Scripture

Slavery remains a deeply emotional and significant topic, especially within the Black community. The reason is clear—slavery was not only a brutal system that inflicted physical harm, but it also caused profound psychological, emotional, and generational trauma. Though today's generations did not experience slavery firsthand, its effects have been passed down through family stories, survival strategies, and cultural behaviors. It is embedded in our collective memory and continues to shape how we perceive and respond to the world around us, especially when we encounter reminders of that painful history.

---

[21] The Constitutions of Oxford (1408), enacted under Archbishop Thomas Arundel, forbade the translation of the Bible into English or the reading of any such translation without ecclesiastical permission. See Anne Hudson, The Premature Reformation (Oxford: Clarendon Press, 1988), 437–440.

Because many of our perspectives are formed not just by personal experience but through what has been passed down, you do not have to have lived through slavery to feel its impact. Its legacy is still very real, evident in economic inequality, systemic racism, and various social disparities that continue to affect people of color today. So, when someone hears about slavery being mentioned in the Bible, it is understandable that they might feel triggered—even if they have not explored what the Bible actually says.

It is important to understand that the concept of slavery in the Bible does not always align with the chattel slavery of the Transatlantic Slave Trade. Biblical slavery was often rooted in economics—what we might call "debt slavery"—where individuals worked to repay debts or survive extreme poverty. According to the Law of Moses, kidnapping and selling people (as was done during the Transatlantic Slave Trade) was strictly forbidden. In fact, the book of Exodus declares that anyone who kidnaps and sells another person must be put to death.[22] There were, however, instances in the Bible where people exploited others for selfish reasons. Still, the Old Testament includes instructions that call for humane treatment of servants. The book of Deuteronomy says:

> *"And when you let him go free from you, you shall not let him go empty-handed. You shall furnish him liberally out of your flock, out of your threshing floor, and out of your winepress. As the LORD your God has blessed you, you shall give to him" (Deuteronomy 15:12–14, ESV).*

[22] Exodus 21:16 (ESV): "Whoever steals a man and sells him, and anyone found in possession of him, shall be put to death."

These kinds of rules show a concern for the dignity and welfare of the individual, even within that system. While the Bible does not explicitly outlaw slavery altogether, it contains numerous passages that regulate it, condemn certain practices, and elevate the value of human life. The New Testament, especially in the writings of Paul, encourages just and fair treatment of servants and emphasizes that all are equal in Christ, whether slave or free. The Bible's references to slavery must be understood within their cultural and historical context. The slavery described in Scripture differs greatly from the racialized, dehumanizing system that shaped American history. That said, the emotional reaction many feel today is valid and rooted in real generational trauma. But by studying the text carefully, without the manipulation of white supremacy, we can separate historical context from misuse and gain a more accurate understanding of what the Bible actually teaches.

Unicorns in the Bible: Myth or Mistranslation?

The Bible mentions unicorns eight times, which often surprises modern readers. When we hear the word "unicorn," we usually picture a mythological white horse with a spiraled horn, something out of a fairy tale. This image has been passed down through generations and reinforced by art, media, and folklore. But what if that imagery was never the Bible's intention? What if this misunderstanding has distorted our interpretation of certain Scriptures? This disconnect is more than just a linguistic quirk—it is a deliberate shift in perception. Because when people read about unicorns in the Bible, their immediate reaction is often disbelief or skepticism. "Unicorns? That proves the Bible is just a book of legends," some might say. But the reality is quite different when you look more closely at historical definitions and original language usage.

In Noah Webster's 1828 Dictionary, the word unicorn is defined as "an animal with one horn; the Monoceros. This name is often applied to the rhinoceros."[23] Here, the unicorn is not some mythical creature; it is actually a rhinoceros—a real, powerful animal. Interestingly, one of the scientific names for the Indian rhinoceros is Rhinoceros unicornis (meaning "one-horned nose-beast"). Another species, the African black rhino, is called Diceros bicornis ("two-horned").[24] Now consider these biblical references:

> *"God brought him forth out of Egypt; he hath as it were the strength of a unicorn: he shall eat up the nations his enemies, and shall break their bones, and pierce them through with his arrows" (Numbers 24:8, KJV).*

> *"But my horn shalt thou exalt like the horn of a unicorn: I shall be anointed with fresh oil" (Psalm 92:10, KJV).*

In both cases, the unicorn is portrayed as strong, powerful, and significant, not the delicate, fantasy-like image we are accustomed to. Yet in many modern Bible translations, the word unicorn has been changed to "wild ox." While an ox is indeed strong, it lacks the

---

[23] Noah Webster, An American Dictionary of the English Language (New York: S. Converse, 1828), s.v. "unicorn." Webster defined the unicorn as "an animal with one horn; the Monoceros. This name is often applied to the rhinoceros."
[24] The Indian rhinoceros (Rhinoceros unicornis) is a single-horned species native to the Indian subcontinent. The African black rhinoceros (Diceros bicornis) is typically characterized by its two horns. However, in some cases, it may lose one of its horns due to injury, fighting, natural wear, or human intervention such as dehorning for conservation purposes.. See International Rhino Foundation, "Species Overview," accessed 2024.

singular imagery and cultural implications tied to the original translation. Why the change? It could be a matter of linguistic evolution. Still, it could also reflect a broader trend: shifting biblical imagery to be more symbolic, less literal, or even less tied to specific regions, such as Africa. If we recognize the unicorn of the Bible as a rhinoceros, we begin to see something powerful. The rhinoceros is native to Africa and India, and that connection ties the biblical world not just to the so-called Middle East, but also to the African continent. This challenges narrow views of biblical geography and reminds us that Africa has played and continues to play a vital role in biblical history. Egypt, Ethiopia, Cush, and other regions of Africa are mentioned throughout Scripture. So why not the rhino?

Image 1: Picture of a one-horned Rhinoceros and its baby.

Image 2: Picture of a two-horned Rhinoceros.

Geography, Identity, and the "Middle East" Narrative

Another reason people struggle to accept the color, culture, and identity of the people in the Bible is due to geographic labeling. The global system has fueled this confusion by labeling the central locations of many biblical events as the "Middle East," which shifts the focus toward an Arabian (rather than African) demographic. Yet the term "Middle East" was coined only in the 1850s by the British India Office.[25] Before that, this region was known by other names. Some suggest it was referred to as Northeast Africa or simply as part of the broader African and Asian landmass.

Two major changes helped reinforce this misleading narrative: renaming the region and altering its geography. Ancient maps show

[25] The term "Middle East" may have originated in the 1850s in the British India Office. It was popularized in 1902 by American naval strategist Alfred Thayer Mahan in his article "The Persian Gulf and International Relations," published in the National Review. See Roderic H. Davison, "Where Is the Middle East?" Foreign Affairs 38, no. 4 (1960): 665–675.

that this land was once physically connected to Africa. But with the construction of the Suez Canal, an artificial divide was introduced, further supporting the "Middle East" identity and separating it from its African context.[26]

Image 3: Shaded map of the Middle East.

In 1850, the new regional name was introduced. By 1859, construction of the canal was underway. On November 17, 1869, an artificial waterway connecting the Mediterranean Sea to the Red Sea through the Isthmus of Suez was completed and officially opened. Built by the Suez Canal Company between 1859 and 1869, the canal physically divided the land. Where people once could walk directly from Israel into Egypt, they now had to cross a body of water. This

[26] The Suez Canal was constructed between 1859 and 1869 by the Compagnie Universelle du Canal Maritime de Suez, founded by French diplomat Ferdinand de Lesseps. It officially opened on November 17, 1869. See Zachary Karabell, Parting the Desert: The Creation of the Suez Canal (New York: Alfred A. Knopf, 2003).

deliberate geographic separation, orchestrated by powerful interests, was part of a larger strategy to confuse and mislead the masses. However, we must no longer allow the world to distort the truth about who the people of the Bible were and what they looked like.

Image 4: The Suez Canal.

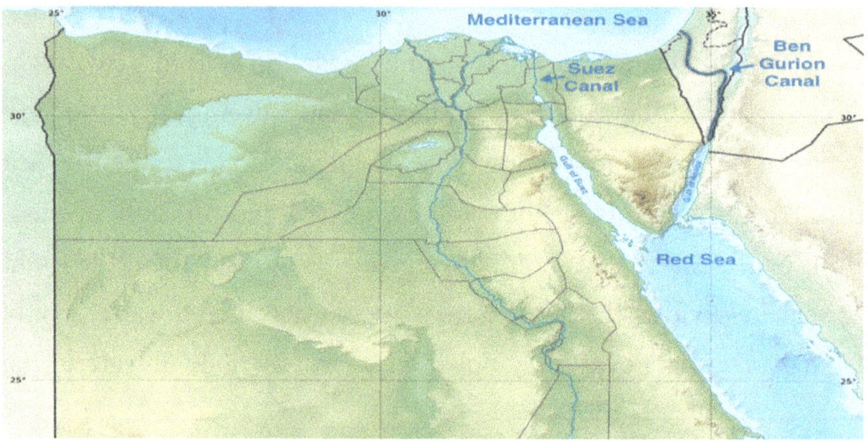

Image 5: Location of the Suez Canal.

From the beginning to the end of the Bible, there is significant evidence that the people of the Bible were melanated, yet so much was done to conceal it. Hollywood also contributed to this by creating movies that depict the people of the Bible either as Europeans or as people of some other culture, but not as Africans. In addition, they understand that when you have people who do not know their identity, whatever images you give them, they will accept as truth. So, Hollywood provides either the image of white supremacy or Euro-mixed ethnicity, and we believe it as fact.

C. McGhee Livers wrote in her book, *Biblical History of Black Mankind*, that in Hebrew, "Adam (Ah-dahm) means swarthy, dusky, dark-skinned, like a shadow."[27] Many people say the Garden of Eden was in Africa. Personally, I do not doubt it. However, no one truly knows where the Garden of Eden was located. Because of the Flood and the shifting of landmasses over time, it has likely disappeared or been drastically altered. Nevertheless, there are other ways to conclude that the Bible is a book centered on African geography.

To name a few: Eden's rivers flow through areas linked to Africa. Egypt, Cush (Ethiopia), and Libya are central in both the Old and New Testaments. The Ethiopian eunuch is one of the first recorded converts to Christianity. African theologians like Tertullian and Augustine shaped early Christian doctrine.[28] Several Hebrew

---

[27] C. McGhee Livers, Biblical History of Black Mankind (Indianapolis: Shahar Institute & Publishing, 1999). Livers, a Greek and Hebrew language scholar and Summa Cum Laude graduate of Indiana University, translates the Hebrew Adam (Ah-dahm) as "swarthy, dusky, dark-skinned, like a shadow."

[28] Tertullian (c. 155–240 AD) and Augustine of Hippo (354–430 AD), both from North Africa, were foundational figures in early Christian theology. Tertullian contributed significantly to the development of Latin Christian terminology, including the concept of the Trinity, while Augustine's works—such as *Confessions*

patriarchs had relationships with women from African tribes. Abraham fathered children with Hagar and Keturah, both of whom are believed to have been of African (Hamitic) descent. Moses married Zipporah, a woman from Ethiopia. Jacob also had children with two handmaidens from African lineage, and their sons became the patriarchs of two tribes of Israel.

Some might say, "Color doesn't matter." But if that were true, why was so much effort put into changing the color, names, and culture of the people in the Bible? Clearly, color mattered so much that people rewrote history and spread falsehoods to keep the world from discovering the truth about the color, culture, and identity of the Bible's characters and other nations with which those characters interacted.

Science, Faith, and the Limits of Human Knowledge

I do believe that science should confirm the Bible. However, in many instances, science is used to try to disprove it. This is another reason why many people do not believe. If you press deeply into mathematics, you'll discover that no matter how refined or advanced a system becomes, there will always be truths that lie beyond its reach—realities that cannot be proven within the system itself. When you turn to biology (the study of life, evolution, and genetics), you find remarkable progress and breathtaking discoveries, yet even there, significant gaps remain. There are questions about origin, complexity, and consciousness that science continues to wrestle with but has not fully answered.

---

and City of God—profoundly shaped Western Christian doctrine. See: The Story of Christianity, Volume 1; Early Christian Doctrines.

Step into physics and the study of the universe, and the same pattern emerges. Despite sophisticated theories and models, we still cannot fully explain the fundamental constants that make life possible. These values appear finely tuned, yet their origin remains a mystery. And even if science could one day map out every particle, every force, and every law governing the universe, it would still be confined to the natural world—unable to cross into the realm of ultimate purpose or first cause.

This is the boundary line of science. It is not a flaw, but a limit. Science is powerful, but it is not all-encompassing. It can describe what is, but it cannot ultimately answer why it is. And this is why the question of God has never been eliminated—it has simply remained beyond the reach of scientific tools. Not disproven, but untouched by the methods designed only to measure the physical.

Science is built to study the natural world, things that can be observed, measured, tested, and repeated. God, by definition, is supernatural, beyond time, space, and matter. Because of this, the Most-High is outside the scope of scientific inquiry. Science cannot disprove what it is not designed to detect. Not being able to measure something does not mean it is not real. Just because science has not found physical proof of God does not mean God does not exist. That would be like saying dark matter did not exist before we discovered evidence for it. Questions of meaning, morality, and ultimate purpose are beyond the reach of science. Many brilliant minds, such as Sir Isaac Newton, Albert Einstein, and Francis Collins, saw no conflict between science and belief in a higher power.[29] Some saw science as a way to explore the mind of God.

Science cannot disprove God because God is not a testable scientific hypothesis. The tools of science are not made to detect or refute a supernatural Creator. That is why belief in God ultimately remains a matter of faith, philosophy, and personal conviction, not laboratory proof. However, because of humanity's intellect, many try to use science to oppose the truths of the Bible. Let us take a look at a few examples.

After World War II, the United States launched Operation Paperclip. This secret intelligence program brought over 1,600 German scientists, engineers, and technicians to the U.S. to work for the government.[30] Many were formerly part of the Nazi regime or the SS. The objective was to advance technology beyond the reach of the Soviet Union and other adversaries. Some of these men helped create our space program, but the broader effect, I believe, was to steer humanity's mindset away from the order of God and belief in God, toward looking to mere men for sovereignty and knowledge. So now we hold the news stations in high regard for their understanding, yet they constantly exaggerate and recycle the same narratives. We

---

[29] Isaac Newton wrote extensively on theology alongside his scientific work, reflecting his belief in a rational Creator. Albert Einstein often spoke of a sense of cosmic order and described belief in a higher intelligence through what he called a "cosmic religious feeling." Francis Collins, former director of the National Institutes of Health, openly affirms Christian faith in his book The Language of God. See: The Language of God; Einstein: His Life and Universe; Never at Rest: A Biography of Isaac Newton.

[30] Operation Paperclip was a secret U.S. intelligence program that recruited more than 1,600 German scientists, engineers, and technicians from former Nazi Germany between 1945 and 1959. See Annie Jacobsen, Operation Paperclip: The Secret Intelligence Program to Bring Nazi Scientists to America (New York: Little, Brown, 2014).

believe what we are fed, even if a Nazi scientist formulated it, and we dare not challenge what we are told, because they have mastered the art of persuasion.

Science estimates that the Earth is billions of years old using methods such as radiometric dating of rocks and astronomical observations.[31] However, many who hold to a literal interpretation of the Bible believe the Earth is about 6,000 years old, based on genealogies and historical records found in Scripture. Looking at the Earth's timeline through this lens places Genesis as the literal start of history. In the lost book of Adam and Eve, it states in Chapter 42 that Michael the archangel appeared to Seth (the son of Adam) and said to him:[32]

> *"When five thousand five hundred years have been fulfilled, then will come upon earth the most beloved king Christ, the son of God, to revive the body of Adam and with him to revive the bodies of the dead. He Himself, the Son of God, when He comes will be baptized in the river of Jordan, and when He hath come out of the water of Jordan, then He will anoint from the oil of mercy all that believe in Him. And the oil of mercy shall be for generation to generation for those who are ready to be born again."*

---

[31] Modern scientific estimates place the age of the Earth at approximately 4.54 billion years, based on radiometric dating of rocks and meteorites, as well as astronomical observations of planetary formation. See: United States Geological Survey; National Aeronautics and Space Administration; The Age of the Earth.
[32] The Vita Adae et Evae (Life of Adam and Eve), also known as the Conflict of Adam and Eve with Satan, is an ancient pseudepigraphal text not included in the biblical canon. The passage cited is from Chapter 42 of the text. See M. D. Johnson, "Life of Adam and Eve," in Old Testament Pseudepigrapha, ed. James H. Charlesworth (Garden City, NY: Doubleday, 1985), 2:249–295.

The book of Nicodemus also quotes, in Chapter 14, that after five thousand and five hundred years, Christ will come to earth to raise the human body of Adam again, and at the same time raise the bodies of the dead, and issue His mercy on all who believe in Him.[33]

In the ancient world, time was often measured using different systems. One of the earliest methods was Anno Mundi ("Year of the World"), which calculated time beginning from the Creation or, in some traditions, from the Fall of Man. This system attempted to trace human history directly from the Genesis account, grounding the calendar in a biblical timeline.[34]

As time progressed, Anno Mundi was eventually replaced by BC ("Before Christ") and later by AD ("Anno Domini," Latin for "in the year of our Lord"), which shifted the global reckoning of time around the birth of Christ. Still, these systems have been known to contain errors. Rome was founded approximately 722 years before the reign of Gaius Octavius, who would later become known as Caesar Augustus, the first emperor of the Roman Empire.[35] His reign marked a pivotal moment in both world history and biblical prophecy, as it

---

33 The Gospel of Nicodemus (also called the Acts of Pilate) is a medieval apocryphal text. The passage referenced is from Chapter 14 (in some recensions, Chapter 19). See J. K. Elliott, The Apocryphal New Testament (Oxford: Clarendon Press, 1993), 164–204.

34 Anno Mundi ("Year of the World") is a calendar system that reckons time from the biblical creation of the world. The Septuagint's chronology dates creation to approximately 5500 BC, while the Masoretic Text places it closer to 4000 BC. See Jack Finegan, Handbook of Biblical Chronology, rev. ed. (Peabody, MA: Hendrickson, 1998).

35 The traditional date for the founding of Rome is 753 BC (*ab urbe condita*, "from the founding of the city"). Gaius Octavius, later known as Augustus, emerged as the sole ruler of the Roman world after the Battle of Actium in 31 BC, placing that event approximately 722 years after Rome's founding. Although the title "Augustus" was officially conferred in 27 BC, the chronology surrounding his rise to undisputed authority provides an important historical reference point for dating the events surrounding the birth of Christ (Luke 2:1).

coincided with the birth of Christ. However, if Anno Mundi is indeed the most accurate way to trace humanity's age based on biblical chronology, then the historical timing of Caesar Augustus's reign provides strong confirmation of that timeline. I believe the relationship between Rome's founding and Augustus's reign further strengthens the plausibility of this connection, especially when considered alongside prophetic timelines and scriptural events.

The Septuagint supports Anno Mundi by preserving a continuous, creation-based biblical chronology that measures history from creation. Through its extended genealogies in Genesis, particularly in Chapters 5 and 11, the Septuagint provides specific ages and generational intervals that allow for an unbroken calculation of time from Adam onward. These chronological details form the basis for dating creation to approximately 5,500 BC, which supports the lost book of Adam and Eve and the book of Nicodemus's prophecy about the coming Christ. This framework was widely accepted in the early church. Because the Septuagint was commonly read in synagogues and used by early Christians, its timeline shaped how biblical history was understood and recorded, reinforcing Anno Mundi as a Scripture-derived method of reckoning time rather than a later-imposed system.[36]

The Septuagint, used by the early church and Orthodox traditions, was considered one of the most important translations of the Hebrew Bible. With the expansion of Alexander the Great and the spread of

---

[36] The Septuagint (LXX) is a Greek translation of the Hebrew Bible produced in the 3rd–2nd centuries BC in Alexandria, Egypt. It was widely used in Hellenistic Jewish communities and became the primary Old Testament text of the early Christian church. See Karen H. Jobes and Moisés Silva, Invitation to the Septuagint (Grand Rapids: Baker Academic, 2000).

the Greek Empire, many Hebrews became increasingly Hellenized. For many Hebrews, Greek replaced Hebrew as their primary language, necessitating a Greek translation of the Scriptures.
While these calculations cannot be confirmed with absolute certainty, they point us back to something we can confirm: the prophetic Word of God. In Daniel 7, the Prophet Daniel foresaw a series of world empires, with the final and most terrifying beast symbolizing a powerful and corrupt system that would arise on the earth. Many scholars believe this beast represents Rome, not just the empire in its ancient form, but a continuation of Roman principles and systems that persist even in modern governance and global structures.[37]

So, while exact dates and measurement systems may shift, what remains constant is that biblical prophecy continues to align with world history in astonishing ways. Whether through the lens of Anno Mundi, the rise of Rome, or the fulfillment of messianic prophecy during the reign of Caesar Augustus, it is clear that God has a sovereign timetable, and all of history is unfolding right on schedule. In the end, the earth's chronological age cannot be proven with certainty, but it certainly does not appear to be millions of years old if we are going by the biblical record.

Science often denies the possibility of miracles described in the Bible, claiming they defy the laws of physics, biology, and logic. For instance, the idea of Christ performing supernatural acts such as walking on water, raising the dead, or being born of a virgin is dismissed by many in the scientific community as implausible. Yet,

---

[37] Daniel 7:7–8, 23–25. Many scholars, both ancient and modern, have interpreted the fourth beast as representing the Roman Empire. See John J. Collins, Daniel, Hermeneia Commentary Series (Minneapolis: Fortress Press, 1993).

ironically, the entertainment industry, particularly Hollywood, is more open to the supernatural than many modern Christians. From blockbuster films involving time travel, spiritual realms, resurrection, and angelic or demonic beings, it is clear that popular culture has embraced the possibility of the supernatural even as mainstream science resists it.

One of the most disputed biblical miracles is the virgin birth of Christ. Science argues that it is biologically impossible for a virgin to conceive. However, Scripture provides context that expands beyond natural limitations. In Genesis 6, the Bible records an extraordinary event in which "sons of God" (often interpreted as fallen angels) had relations with human women, resulting in giants and mighty beings of renown known as the Nephilim.[38] This account, although mysterious, demonstrates that the Bible has always included narratives involving supernatural interaction between heavenly beings and humanity.

Interestingly, the virgin birth is not unique to Christianity. Variations of virgin conception appear in other ancient religions and mythologies, indicating that such a concept has long fascinated humanity. Moreover, there are modern-day reports of people experiencing disturbing phenomena in which they wake up feeling as though something has engaged with them sexually during sleep. These experiences are often attributed to an incubus or a succubus. According to Encyclopedia Britannica, an incubus is a male demon

---

[38] Genesis 6:1–4. The identity of the "sons of God" (Hebrew: bene ha'elohim) has been debated throughout church history. The interpretation that they were fallen angels is found in 1 Enoch 6–16, Jubilees 5:1, and among early church fathers such as Justin Martyr and Clement of Alexandria. See Michael S. Heiser, The Unseen Realm (Bellingham, WA: Lexham Press, 2015).

believed to have sexual intercourse with sleeping women, while the female counterpart, a succubus, targets men.[39]

Though science seeks to explain or dismiss the legitimacy of such experiences, recurring themes across ancient texts, religious beliefs, and modern testimonies suggest that the spiritual realm is far more complex and active than we often acknowledge. The Bible never shies away from this reality, and perhaps it is time for believers to reclaim a deeper understanding of the supernatural elements of their faith, rather than letting Hollywood or secular narratives define them. We must remember that science and the Bible serve different purposes and answer different questions. Science seeks to explain how the natural world works, while the Bible reveals why we exist and who is behind it all. Using science to try to disprove the Bible is like using a microscope to measure love; it is the wrong tool for the task. The truths of Scripture speak to the heart, soul, and purpose of humanity, areas science can observe but never fully explain. Rather than seeing the two as enemies, we should recognize that science can complement faith, but it should never be used to erase it. The Bible is not a science textbook; it is God's Word, offering eternal truths that science alone can never reach.

Translations, Variations, and Perceived Contradictions

Another reason many people struggle to believe the Word of God is due to perceived conflicts within Scripture. It is important to understand that the Bible has gone through many translations over

---

[39] "Incubus," Encyclopedia Britannica, accessed 2024. An incubus is described in medieval European folklore as a male demon believed to engage in sexual activity with sleeping women. The female counterpart is called a succubus.

time. Originally written in Hebrew, Aramaic, and Greek, it was later translated into Latin and then English. With each translation, wording can shift, and meanings may seem altered. For example, John 14:2 in the King James Version says, *"In my father's house are many mansions,"* while the New International Version translates it as, *"My Father's house has many rooms."*[40] Why the difference between "mansions" and "rooms"? These changes often stem from language evolution, cultural context, or translation choices, but they can cause confusion and lead people to question the Bible's consistency.

Many people, when they encounter what appears to be a contradiction or inconsistency, quickly dismiss the entire Bible as false. This is often rooted in a misunderstanding. Some assume that if the Bible is truly God's Word, it must have zero variation or translation differences. But translation is not the same as error. The core message of Scripture remains intact, even if wording shifts slightly between versions. Rejecting the entire Bible over such issues is like discarding a priceless letter because the envelope has changed. It is crucial to seek understanding, not just surface-level interpretation. Another important thing to understand about the Bible is that being inspired by God does not mean God Himself directly wrote every word. God revealed some parts to specific writers, the Holy Spirit inspired others, and some sections are historical records written from human perspectives. The Bible is a collection of writings from multiple authors, each with a unique voice

---

[40] Compare John 14:2 in the King James Version ("mansions") with the New International Version ("rooms"). The underlying Greek word is monai, which can mean "dwelling places" or "rooms." See D. A. Carson, The Gospel According to John, Pillars New Testament Commentary (Grand Rapids: Eerdmans, 1991), 489.

and perspective. That is why it is important to discern between literal, prophetic, and metaphorical language. Just because eyewitness accounts may vary in detail does not mean the event did not happen. Different perspectives can still point to the same truth.

Words and phrases evolve, and their meanings depend on the society of the day. Many people have abandoned their faith not just because of the biblical issues I have pointed out, but also for other reasons. Some have been disillusioned by pastors who have been exposed as hypocrites. Others were following men instead of truly following the Word of God. Some carried unanswered questions for years. As they grew in knowledge and uncovered the historical lies that had once masked the truth, their beliefs began to unravel. However, to understand the Bible, you will have to understand that it was oral information handed down over time, that it was written at different times rather than exactly at the time of the event, and that it was written based on perception. Now, it is worth noting that in every story or piece of information handed down through history, one can find a discrepancy, but that does not mean we throw it all out.

I BELIEVE THE BIBLE—and the things that I question, I research to find the truth. The Apostle Paul said to Timothy, *"Study to show thyself approved unto God, a workman that needeth not to be ashamed, rightly dividing the word of truth" (2 Timothy 2:15, KJV).* One way to affirm the Bible's legitimacy is through historical and archaeological evidence. Over the years, countless archaeological discoveries have corroborated the historical accuracy of the Bible.

The Dead Sea Scrolls: Discovered in the late 1940s, these ancient manuscripts include portions of the Old Testament dating back to the third century BC. They have shown that the Bible's texts have been transmitted with remarkable accuracy over the centuries.[41]

Archaeological Sites: Excavations at sites such as Jericho, Jerusalem, and other biblical locations have unearthed evidence that aligns with biblical accounts. These findings support the Bible's historical reliability and give us confidence that the events recorded in Scripture truly happened.

Another powerful testimony to the Bible's legitimacy is its prophetic accuracy. The Bible contains numerous prophecies that have been fulfilled in remarkable detail. Consider the prophecies about Christ:

Born of a Virgin: Isaiah 7:14 prophesied that the Messiah would be born of a virgin, a prophecy fulfilled in Matthew 1:22–23.[42]

Born in Bethlehem: Micah 5:2 foretold that the Messiah would be born in Bethlehem, a prophecy fulfilled in Matthew 2:1–6.[43]

The Suffering Servant: Isaiah 53 vividly describes Christ's suffering and crucifixion, written centuries before His birth.[44]

---

[41] The Dead Sea Scrolls were discovered between 1947 and 1956 in caves near Qumran on the northwest shore of the Dead Sea. They include the oldest known manuscripts of the Hebrew Bible, dating back to the 3rd century BC. See James C. VanderKam, The Dead Sea Scrolls Today, 2nd ed. (Grand Rapids: Eerdmans, 2010).

[42] Matthew 1:22–23 (KJV): "Now all this was done, that it might be fulfilled which was spoken of the Lord by the prophet, saying, 'Behold, a virgin shall be with child, and shall bring forth a son, and they shall call his name Emmanuel,' which being interpreted is, God with us." This passage affirms the fulfillment of the prophecy found in Isaiah 7:14.

[43] Matthew 2:1–6 (KJV) records the birth of Jesus in Bethlehem during the reign of Herod the king and cites the prophecy of the Messiah's birthplace, stating, "And thou Bethlehem, in the land of Juda, art not the least among the princes of Juda..." This passage reflects the fulfillment of the prophecy found in Micah 5:2.

[44] Isaiah 53, often called the "Suffering Servant" passage, describes in vivid detail the rejection, suffering, and sacrificial death of the Messiah—written approximately 700 years before the birth of Christ.

These prophecies and their fulfillment demonstrate that the Bible's messages are not mere coincidences but divinely inspired revelations. Beyond historical and prophetic evidence, the Bible's transformative power testifies to its legitimacy.[45] The Bible has the power to change lives. It convicts us of sin, offers us the message of salvation, and guides us in righteous living. Countless individuals throughout history have testified to the life-changing impact of engaging with Scripture.

The Bible is more than a religious book. It is a testimony of liberation, resilience, justice, and hope that speaks powerfully to the Black experience. Throughout its pages, we see God siding with the oppressed, lifting the brokenhearted, and calling His people to freedom. From the Hebrew slaves in Egypt to the early church suffering under Roman rule, the Bible tells the story of people who, like us, endured hardship and overcame through faith. It reminds us that we are not forgotten or forsaken, but deeply seen and valued by a God who is just, compassionate, and near to the broken.

For Black and Brown people around the world, especially in the context of systemic injustice and historical trauma, the Bible offers more than comfort; it offers truth, dignity, and a spiritual legacy that cannot be erased. Our ancestors found strength in its promises when all else was stripped away, and it continues to be a source of empowerment, identity, and vision for a better future. To believe the Bible is not to abandon our culture or history, but to embrace a faith that affirms our worth and calls us to walk boldly in purpose, justice,

---

45 Hebrews 4:12 (NLT): "For the word of God is alive and powerful. It is sharper than the sharpest two-edged sword."

and love. Do not believe the hype—the Bible does not oppress and enslave us. When we fully understand, we see that it actually liberates and empowers us!

CHAPTER TWO

Image & Likeness

As we prepare to dive a little deeper, it's important to understand that, for true progress to occur, we must be willing to engage in uncomfortable conversations. The truth is, in His infinite wisdom and sovereignty, God has the power to take what the enemy intends for evil and turn it for good. Yes, He chose Israel as His treasured possession above all nations, and yes, the Gentiles were often regarded in Scripture as heathens. Yet because the Hebrews rejected the Messiah, the door of salvation was opened, allowing the Gentiles to be included in the blessings of the Gospel.

Yahshua Himself declared in John 10:16, *"And other sheep I have, which are not of this fold: them also I must bring, and they shall hear my voice; and there shall be one fold, and one shepherd."*[46] God's ways are higher than our ways, and His thoughts far above our thoughts. His ultimate plan has always been that all who believe in and accept the truth would have the right to eternal life. Therefore, while this book may reveal truths that are sometimes uncomfortable, its ultimate purpose is to present the truth that leads to freedom. As Yahshua said in John 8:32, *"And ye shall know the truth, and the truth shall make you free."*[47] The truth may sting, but it also has the power to heal and bring freedom. So, let's dive in.

The question surrounding identity is one of the most pivotal questions of today's generation. We live in a time where identity is

---

[46] John 10:16 (KJV).
[47] John 8:32 (KJV).

constantly being challenged, distorted, and redefined. Many people struggle with questions like, "Who am I?" What is my purpose? Where do I belong? Everyone is searching, trying to find their way in this society. Some are trying to figure out their ancestral history, some are trying to discover their purpose, and some are trying to reach a place where their dreams and visions are fulfilled, but it is all centered on identity. Identity is important. It defines who we are and helps others define us. If you do not know how important it is, try leaving the country and returning without proper identification. Try getting stopped at a roadblock without your license. Try getting a job without an ID. Identity is who we are and what we are.

Many of us struggle to understand who we are, what our purpose is, what our calling is, and how to get to the place God has destined for us—we face an identity crisis. This crisis can be traced back to the beginning, in the Garden. The serpent challenged Adam and Eve to eat something that would make them "as gods," but the problem is that they were already like God, in the sense that they were made in the image and likeness of God. The enemy tempted them by making them feel inferior. He tempted them with the desire for something higher, a direct challenge to their identity.

The concept of identity has undergone a profound transformation over the past century. In ancient times, a person's sense of self was deeply rooted in family, social class, and occupation. Nowadays, all that has changed. People look to iconic men and women for identity. They search for materialistic things. They look for themselves in money or status, in sex, or in fame. Some try to find happiness in drinking, clubbing, and even drugs.

They even mask themselves in religiosity, having a form of godliness, but denying the power thereof.

I believe that, in today's world, the constant presence of social media platforms keeps us in a perpetual state of comparison—reminding us, day and night, of what we are missing out on and how we do not measure up. Social media forces us to stack our everyday reality against others' curated, polished, and filtered highlight reels. People are wondering who they really are and why they exist without going to the One who created them. To understand the details of creation, you must go to its Creator. And I want you to know it was not the ancestors, not the universe, and not some cosmic accident. It was the Most-High. He formed you, and He created you on purpose—with purpose!

Just as He told the prophet in Jeremiah 1:5, *"Before I formed thee in the belly I knew thee; and before thou camest forth out of the womb I sanctified thee, and I ordained thee a prophet unto the nations."*[48] God knew you before you ever entered this world. He destined you to be here and gave you a purpose. Whether your purpose seems great or small, it is still a purpose, and purpose is the foundation of all achievement and success. It is not God's desire that we lose ourselves, but that we become our true selves. And it is important to know that if you do not allow God to mold you into the creation He intends, then you limit your true potential in life.

---

[48] Jeremiah 1:5 (KJV).

An identity crisis is a period of confusion and doubt surrounding one's sense of self.[49] While everyone's experience of identity crisis can differ, the symptoms are prevalent: a sense of disconnection from one's thoughts, emotions, or physical self; persistent anxiety, stress, fear, or episodes of panic; mental confusion and a lack of clarity; feeling directionless, lost, or uncertain about the next steps; questioning personal values, beliefs, goals, and overall way of life; and deep self-criticism or self-hatred, often expressed through destructive thoughts or behaviors. This is the enemy's tactic and strategy. He always attacks identity.

The Gospel of Matthew, Chapter 3, introduces John the Baptist, a fiery preacher in the wilderness of Judea, calling people to repent, for the kingdom of heaven is near. John is known for his simple camel 's-hair clothing and his diet of locusts and wild honey. Crowds from Jerusalem, Judea, and the region of the Jordan came to him to confess their sins and be baptized. John makes it clear that his baptism is with water, but someone greater is coming (Yahshua the Messiah), who will baptize with the Holy Spirit and fire. He describes Yahshua as one who will bring both judgment and purification. The chapter ends with Yahshua coming to John to be baptized. Though John hesitates, Yahshua insists it is necessary "to fulfill all righteousness." As Yahshua is baptized, the heavens open, the Spirit of God descends like a dove, and a voice from heaven declares, *"This*

---

49 Erik H. Erikson, "Identity: Youth and Crisis" (New York: W. W. Norton & Company, 1968), 16–22.

is my beloved Son, in whom I am well pleased."[50] This was not just a statement; this was an establishment of identity.

This is what a father does—he speaks identity. Within the patriarchal family structure, a father's words (whether spoken as a declaration or a prophecy) carried weight and often shaped reality. What we must understand is this: fathers impart identity to their children. The father's voice has always held profound significance, setting the course and casting the vision for future generations. This is precisely why, throughout history and across generations, there has been a relentless effort, both spiritual and societal, to remove the father from the center of the family structure. Because when a true father is present, he speaks vision, purpose, and identity into his children. And a generation grounded in identity becomes a generation marked by strength, confidence, and unstoppable progress.

The Gospel of Matthew, Chapter 4, tells us that Yahshua was led by the Spirit into the wilderness to be tempted by the devil. After fasting for forty days and forty nights, He entered that moment physically weakened and deeply hungry, setting the stage for a profound spiritual confrontation. The devil said to Him, *"If thou be the Son of God, command that these stones be made bread" (Matthew 4:3).*[51]

It is important to recognize what just happened before this moment. Christ had just been baptized by John the Baptist, and a voice from heaven declared, *"This is My beloved Son, in whom I am well*

---

[50] Matthew 3:13–17 (KJV). The baptism of Yahshua by John the Baptist in the Jordan River marks the public inauguration of His earthly ministry and the divine affirmation of His identity as the Son of God.

[51] Matthew 4:3 (KJV): "And when the tempter came to him, he said, If thou be the Son of God, command that these stones be made bread." This marks the beginning of Christ's temptation in the wilderness following His baptism.

pleased" (Matthew 3:17).[52] God had publicly affirmed Christ's identity. Yet, immediately afterward, He is led into the wilderness, where the enemy questions that very identity: "If You are the Son of God..." Is that not how the enemy often works? He challenges what the Most-High has already confirmed. He tries to sow doubt where God has already spoken truth. Just like Christ, we are often tempted to prove what God has already validated in us. The enemy whispers lies to make us question our worth, our calling, and our identity, but his strategy has not changed: he aims to undermine God's word by twisting it just enough to make us second-guess ourselves. But here is the truth we must hold on to: if the Most-High has spoken it, that settles it. We do not need to prove what God has already approved. Our identity is not found in performance or proof; it is rooted in the Word and will of God.

The wilderness is a place that challenges your identity. In both a biblical and symbolic sense, the wilderness represents a season or place of testing, isolation, and spiritual confrontation. One of the clearest examples is found in the children of Israel. Though they had been freed physically, they still carried the mindset of enslaved people, not children of the Most-High, and that mindset was exposed again and again in the wilderness. God had called Israel to be His chosen people, a holy nation.[53] But in the wilderness, they struggled to live out that calling. Idolatry, rebellion, and complaining showed that they had not fully embraced their identity or purpose. The

---

[52] Matthew 3:16–17 (KJV) records the baptism of Jesus by John the Baptist, in which the heavens opened, the Spirit of God descended like a dove, and a voice from heaven declared, "This is my beloved Son, in whom I am well pleased."
[53] Exodus 19:5–6 (KJV): "And ye shall be unto me a kingdom of priests, and a holy nation."

wilderness exposed the gap between who God said they were and what they still believed about themselves. It was a place where the old identity (slavery, fear, dependence on Egypt) had to die, so that a new identity (sons, warriors, worshippers) could emerge.

Going back to the Gospel of Matthew, Chapter 4: The enemy, in tempting Yahshua, did not attack Yahshua's power or ability first; he went straight for His identity. The wilderness, then, becomes the battleground where identity is questioned and tested. Symbolically, the wilderness strips away external validation, comfort, and support systems, forcing you to confront whether you truly believe what God has said about you. It is not the place that gives you your identity, but it is where the identity you have been given is proven. Spiritually speaking, the wilderness asks: Will you still believe what God declared in the light when you are standing in the shadows? It is in these challenging seasons that false identities fall away, and the truth of who you are in God is refined, affirmed, and strengthened.

> *"Again, the devil taketh him up into an exceeding high mountain, and sheweth him all the kingdoms of the world, and the glory of them; and saith unto him, All these things will I give thee, if thou wilt fall down and worship me" (Matthew 4:8–9, KJV).*

This passage is not just about temptation; it is a revelation of authority, kingdoms, and spiritual warfare. The very fact that Satan could offer "all the kingdoms of the world" suggests that he held a degree of influence or dominion over them. That dominion was not self-created; it was given through humanity's fall and disobedience. And here lies the deeper issue: when we talk about earthly power, politics, or leadership, we must ask, what kingdom does it serve? You can cast your vote, campaign, or choose your leaders, but behind every throne lies a spiritual influence. The question is not just who is in charge, but what spirit or kingdom they are aligned with.

Paul reinforces this when he writes, *"For we wrestle not against flesh and blood, but against principalities, against powers, against the rulers of the darkness of this world, and against spiritual wickedness in high places" (Ephesians 6:12, KJV).* This is not a battle of left versus right, the donkey versus the elephant, or Democrat versus Republican. It is light versus darkness, Kingdom versus kingdom. Discernment is critical. Do not just look at policies; look at fruit. Do not just hear speeches; discern the spirit. Because in the end, only one Kingdom will stand, and it is not built by human hands.

Sun Tzu states in his book *The Art of War*, "If you know the enemy and know yourself, you need not fear the result of a hundred battles. If you know yourself but not the enemy, for every victory gained, you will also suffer a defeat. If you know neither the enemy nor yourself, you will succumb in every battle."[54] Is it not remarkable that the one time in the Scriptures where we see Yahshua and Satan in direct conflict, it is over identity? This is important because there is a full-blown attack on identity, and if we are not sober and vigilant, we will end up confused, and confusion leads to compromise. That was Israel's issue. God repeatedly warned them, saying, *"When you enter the land I promised your forefathers, do not forget the Lord your God, the One who brought you out of bondage and led you to this*

---

[54] Sun Tzu, The Art of War, trans. Lionel Giles (London: Luzac, 1910), Chapter 3, p. 18. Sun Tzu (c. 544–496 BC) was a Chinese military strategist and philosopher whose treatise remains one of the most influential works on strategy ever written.

place."[55] When God repeats Himself, it is not casual; it is critical. His warnings are never empty. However, at the heart of every evil temptation is a challenge to what God has said about you, a question of who you are, and a distortion of how the Most-High sees you.

When the enemy wants to create an identity crisis in your life, he always starts with deception. This is not a new tactic—it is ancient, strategic, and subtle. We saw it in the Garden with Eve, when the serpent twisted God's words, causing her to question what God had really said. We saw it again with Christ, when Satan tempted Yahshua to prove who He was, even though God had already declared, "*This is my beloved Son.*" And we see it repeatedly with Israel, a nation chosen and set apart by God, yet constantly struggling to remember who they were.

Israel's deception came in many forms. First, there was idolatry through foreign influence. Surrounded by nations that worshiped false gods, Israel was drawn into their practices, mainly through intermarriage, which slowly led their hearts away from the Most-High. Then there was paganism: instead of obeying God's command to drive out the Canaanites, they tolerated and eventually adopted their customs and religious systems. Corrupt leadership also played a major role, as false prophets and ungodly rulers rose, claiming to speak for God while leading the people further into darkness. And perhaps most damaging of all was fear and lack of faith. Time and time again, Israel doubted God's promises, allowing fear to drive their decisions rather than trust.

---

55 Deuteronomy 6:10-12 (KJV).

But do not be deceived! Deception is the enemy's calculated weapon to make you forget who you are, what God has said, and how much He loves you. When you lose sight of your identity, you become vulnerable to compromise, confusion, and captivity. Stand firm, stay rooted, and remember: the attack is not just on your mind; it is on your identity.

What Does the Bible Mean When It Says You Are Made in the Image and Likeness of God?

Many people do not interpret this verse literally; they assume there must be a deeper, symbolic meaning. As a result, they believe it does not refer to physical form, color, or function in a literal sense. It is also important to recognize that the Bible is not arranged in chronological order. While the book of Genesis does not explicitly state that Moses wrote it, early church tradition, the Jewish Talmud, and the Hebrew historian Josephus all affirmed that Moses wrote the first five books of the Bible, collectively known as the Pentateuch.[56] Moses likely received much of this historical revelation during the Exodus, particularly when he met with the Most-High on the mountain.

In the Book of Jubilees 1:1–5, God called Moses to Mount Sinai shortly after Israel's exodus from Egypt to receive the tablets of the Law. God's glory covered the mountain for six days, and on the seventh day He spoke to Moses from within the cloud, appearing as a blazing fire. Moses remained on the mountain for forty days and

---

[56] Jewish tradition, the Talmud (Bava Batra 14b), and the historian Josephus (Against Apion 1.8) all attribute authorship of the first five books of the Bible (the Pentateuch or Torah) to Moses. See Roger T. Beckwith, The Old Testament Canon of the New Testament Church (Grand Rapids: Eerdmans, 1985).

nights, during which God revealed to him the laws, commandments, and the history and future of His covenant with Israel.[57] God instructed Moses to write everything down so future generations would know that, despite their sins, He had never abandoned them or His covenant.[58]

> *"And God said, Let us make man in our image, after our likeness: and let them have dominion over the fish of the sea, and over the fowl of the air, and over the cattle, and over all the earth, and over every creeping thing that creepeth upon the earth" (Genesis 1:25–26, KJV).*

Regarding the nature of God, it is worth noting that the early Catholic Church developed the doctrine of the Trinity. Nowhere in Scripture do we find a prophet or teacher explicitly stating that God is three persons. Many accept this idea because it is difficult to comprehend how God could be in Heaven, appear on Earth as Christ, and work through the Holy Spirit simultaneously. In trying to make this understandable, we risk limiting God's true omnipotence and mystery by reducing it to human logic. A helpful way to grasp this

---

[57] The covenant God established with Israel through Moses was a conditional agreement in which Yahweh declared Israel to be His chosen people, and Israel was required to obey His laws and commandments. This covenant included the giving of the Law (Torah), the Ten Commandments, instructions for worship, priesthood, sacrifices, holiness, and civil conduct. God promised blessings, protection, and favor for obedience, while warning of judgment and exile for disobedience. The covenant also pointed forward to the coming Messiah and ultimately to the New Covenant fulfilled through Christ. See Exodus 19:5–6; Exodus 24:3–8; Deuteronomy 28; Jeremiah 31:31–33; Hebrews 8:6–13.

[58] The Book of Jubilees 1:1–5. Jubilees is an ancient Hebrew text, also called "The Little Genesis," dating to approximately the 2nd century BC. It was preserved in the Ethiopian Orthodox canon and among the Dead Sea Scrolls. See James C. VanderKam, The Book of Jubilees (Sheffield: Sheffield Academic Press, 2001).

concept is to consider our own complexity. For example, I can be a father, a son, and a musician—all at once—yet still be one person.

From my perspective, I have come to believe that when the Most-High said, "Let us make man..." in Genesis, God was not speaking to three parts of Himself, but to the heavenly host. Not because He needed help, but because they were created to assist Him. This understanding is supported by verse 27, which says, "So God created man in His own image," not in "their" own image. While God does not need assistance, Scripture shows that He often reveals His intentions to His servants, including the angels and prophets. Understanding this helps us see the consistency and depth of God's character without reducing Him to human logic. The Most-High also said to the heavenly host in Genesis 11 regarding the Tower of Babel, *"Go to, let us go down, and there confound their language, that they may not understand one another's speech" (Genesis 11:7, KJV).*

So, again, I believe that God is addressing the heavenly host who serve in His presence. This is also consistent with some Jewish and scholarly interpretations. It's like when kings often spoke in the presence of their royal court. The text does not imply shared decision-making authority. So, when God speaks with words like "us," it is similar to royal speech, like a king saying, "Let us go to war," though the king leads the charge.

> *"So God created man in his own image, in the image of God created he him; male and female created he them" (Genesis 1:27, KJV).*

This verse stands as a singular, definitive, and complete declaration of God's creative authority. It affirms that humanity was intentionally and divinely crafted in the very image of God (both male and female), highlighting purpose and identity from the very beginning. The Hebrew word for "create" is bara, a term used in Scripture to describe a kind of creation that only God can perform—bringing something into existence out of nothing.[59] Unlike humanity, which can only form, fashion, or rearrange what already exists, bara speaks to a divine power that operates beyond natural limitation. From the opening words of Genesis, we see that the Creator needed no materials, tools, or assistance. He spoke, and reality responded. Humans may invent, build, and innovate, but we have never truly created in the sense of bara. This distinction reveals the Creator's unmatched omnipotence, whose authority extends not only to what exists but to existence itself.

The Hebrew word translated as "image" is *tselem*, which conveys the idea of a visible form or resemblance—something concrete and recognizable, not abstract or mystical.[60] This same term is used in Genesis, where it says, *"When Adam had lived 130 years, he fathered a son in his own likeness, after his image, and named him Seth" (Genesis 5:3, ESV)*. The use of *tselem* here is unmistakable: Adam produced a son who looked like him; his resemblance was clearly seen and passed on. According to Strong's Concordance, *tselem* is a masculine noun that is frequently associated with words like form,

---

59 The Hebrew word bara (ברא) appears approximately fifty times in the Old Testament and is used exclusively with God as the subject, signifying creation ex nihilo—out of nothing. See R. Laird Harris, Gleason L. Archer Jr., and Bruce K. Waltke, Theological Wordbook of the Old Testament (Chicago: Moody Press, 1980), 1:127.

60 The Hebrew word tselem (צלם), Strong's H6754, means "image, likeness, resemblance." It is used in the physical sense in Genesis 5:3, where Adam fathered Seth "in his own likeness, after his image." See James Strong, Strong's Exhaustive Concordance of the Bible (Nashville: Abingdon Press, 1890).

figure, resemblance, and construct—all of which point to something visible and physically evident.

When God made man, He declared that it was "very good." That declaration is not just a statement of quality but a reflection of God's character. God is good, and His creation mirrors His goodness. We can look at this world and see a lot that does not reflect the image of God; we can see much that is wrong. But this verse reminds us that, even beyond the enemy's distortion, what God made was very good.[61] When you see through God's eyes, you do not see the flaws; you see the potential, the beauty, and the divine purpose. You are made in His image, and you carry the imprint of the goodness of God. You are unique. You are fearfully and wonderfully made. That means God skillfully constructed you. Therefore, we must live in a way that reflects the original intent, God's divine goodness!

Personally, I prefer to understand the word "image" more specifically as a resemblance. For example, you may resemble your parents while still having your own identity. Resemblance can be seen in physical traits, character, manner of communication, or even in congruency of thought or behavior. This resemblance can be either exact or simply similar. In Genesis 2:16–22, God told Adam he could eat freely from every tree in the Garden of Eden except the tree of the knowledge of good and evil, warning that disobedience would lead to death. Seeing that it was not good for Adam to be alone, God formed the animals and brought them to Adam to be named, yet none were suitable as a true companion. So, God caused Adam to fall into a deep sleep, took

---

[61] Genesis records that when God finished His work, "God saw everything that he had made, and, behold, it was very good" (Genesis 1:31), revealing that creation originally reflected the goodness and order of God before the Fall.

one of his ribs, and from it created Eve, whom He presented to Adam as his perfect helper and partner.[62] This detail is significant because God chose the only bone in the body that can regenerate, as long as the rib's protective lining (the periosteum) remains intact. Because Eve came from Adam, they both were of the same substance.

Another common misconception is the idea that God is both masculine and feminine, or that because He is spirit, He has no gender. However, when we read the Word of God, we consistently see Him revealed in a masculine nature throughout the Scriptures. The claim that God has no gender seems to be more of a modern theory used to justify or support current gender identity discussions. Yet there is no instance in Scripture where God presents Himself as anything other than masculine. This is significant, especially in light of Revelation, which speaks of the unification between Christ and His bride, the Church. God's titles across the biblical languages, Hebrew, Aramaic, and Greek, are all grammatically masculine. In addition, all pronouns used for God, such as *He, Him,* and *His,* are masculine. Even the Holy Spirit, who is the Spirit of God, is consistently portrayed in masculine terms throughout the Bible.

This masculine portrayal is clear even in tender moments. For example, Isaiah 49:15 compares God's love to a mother's compassion for her nursing child (a deeply nurturing image). Yet, this same God is also described as a mighty warrior in Isaiah 42:13: *"The LORD goes out like a mighty man, like a man of war he stirs up his zeal; he cries*

---

[62] Genesis 2:16–22 (KJV). The rib (Hebrew: tsela) is the only bone in the human body known to regenerate when the periosteum (outer membrane) is left intact. See medical literature on rib regeneration: Mundy et al., "Rib Regeneration: Harnessing the Body's Natural Repair Mechanisms," Journal of Thoracic Disease 7, no. S1 (2015).

out, he shouts aloud, he shows himself mighty against his foes."[63] These descriptions reflect a balance of strength and compassion within a masculine identity, not a genderless or androgynous being. Ultimately, I believe this issue ties directly to the identity crisis many people face today. When we lose clarity about the nature, image, and likeness of our Creator, we inevitably struggle with understanding ourselves. That confusion and insecurity are then reflected in creation itself.

> *"And they were both naked, the man and his wife, and were not ashamed" (Genesis 2:25, KJV).*

Adam and Eve did not need clothing because clothing serves the purpose of covering, and the glory of the Most-High already covered them. There was no reason for shame, as shame arises from sin, the awareness or exposure of one's faults, wrongdoings, or imperfections.

Creation Reveals the Glory of God

Creation is one of the greatest mysteries humanity has ever pondered. From the vastness of the world to the complexity of a single cell, the diversity and intricacy of life point to an intelligent and purposeful Creator. But what is the meaning behind it all? Why did God create the heavens, the earth, and us? When we observe creation, it should inspire us to worship. The beauty and grandeur of the world around us should evoke awe and reverence toward the Creator. Creation was not an accident or a random event; it was a deliberate act by a loving and sovereign God. Every element in creation, from the stars in the sky to the tiniest living creature, reflects God's glory and wisdom.

---

[63] Isaiah 42:13 (ESV).

> *"The heavens declare the glory of God, and the sky above proclaims his handiwork. Day to day pours out speech, and night to night reveals knowledge" (Psalm 19:1–2, ESV).*

In essence, the world is a manifestation of God's glory. Every aspect of creation testifies to the greatness, creativity, and power of God. The beauty and order we observe in the world are a testament to His majesty. So, the purpose of creation is to reveal God's glory, showcase His majesty, and draw our attention to His divine nature. Our existence is not accidental. We were created with intention and purpose. Recognizing that we exist because God willed it gives our lives meaning and direction. The Bible begins with *"In the beginning, God created the heavens and the earth" (Genesis 1:1, KJV).* This powerful and complete statement lays the foundation for understanding that all creation originates from God, with purpose and intent. Everything that exists does so because God willed it into being. Creation is an expression of God's pleasure and sovereign will, and the world, including humanity, was created to fulfill God's divine purposes.

> *"Thou art worthy, O Lord, to receive glory and honour and power: for thou hast created all things, and for thy pleasure they are and were created" (Revelation 4:11, KJV).*

Humanity, created in the image of God, was designed to engage in fellowship with Him by reflecting His divine image. People were made to glorify God by expressing their unique capacities through their minds, hearts, and wills. With their minds, they were to understand God; with their hearts, they were to love Him; and with their wills, they were to choose obedience to God. However, God did not create humans as robots; this would not bring true glory to Him. The freedom to choose, even at the risk of disobedience, was essential to this relationship. In His sovereign wisdom and purpose, God granted this freedom, which has at times been used as an opportunity for sin, though He Himself is not the author of sin.

The ultimate purpose of creation is deeply connected with God's love. He created the world not only to display His glory but also to establish a relationship with His creation. The very act of creation is an expression of God's love, and the sending of Christ into the world is the ultimate demonstration of that love. Knowing that the Creator of the world loves us should fill us with confidence and hope. We are valuable in God's eyes, and His love for us is the foundation of our existence. Moreover, we were created to enjoy a relationship with God. In the Garden of Eden, Adam and Eve walked with God in close fellowship. Although sin disrupted this relationship, through Christ the Messiah, God made a way for us to be reconciled to Him.

Our purpose is not only to live in relationship with God but also to accomplish the good works He has planned for us and to worship Him. Just as every product has a purpose defined by its creator, our purpose is defined by God, not by ourselves. All of creation is meant to praise the Most-High. The sun, moon, stars, and all living creatures are part of a grand symphony of worship that honors the Creator. Humanity, made in God's image, plays a unique role in this worship. We are called to worship God not only with our words but with our lives. Everything we do (whether it is our work, relationships, or hobbies) can be an act of worship if done with the right heart. We are called to live lives that glorify God in all aspects.

Though marred by sin, creation is part of God's redemptive plan. It longs for the day when it will be restored, just as we do. The purpose of creation is not only to reveal God's glory but also to direct us to the hope of redemption through Christ. God has provided a perfect way for us to be reconciled to Him, walk with Him, and overcome sin's power through the finished work of Christ on the cross and the many blessings we have in Him. We live in a broken world, but this is not the end. God is actively working to redeem and restore all things. As followers of the Messiah, we have the hope of a new creation where there will be no more pain, suffering, or death.

In this context, salvation through Christ can be understood in three phases: in the past, through faith in Christ, we are saved from the penalty of sin; in the present, we are being delivered from the power of sin as we walk in faith and fellowship with Him; and in the future, when He returns, we will be saved from the very presence of sin. Therefore, we cannot blame the Most-High. He has provided more than enough to address our sin problem, even giving us His Son. For humanity, the purpose of our creation is particularly significant. Genesis 1:27 says, *"So God created mankind in his own image."*[64] Being made in God's image gives us a unique identity and responsibility. We are called to reflect God's character in our lives through love, justice, mercy, and righteousness. This means living in a way that honors God and serves others.

---

[64] Genesis 1:27 (KJV).

What Is God's Image?

Understanding the geographical area would imply a region where the people of the Bible would have needed melanin to survive the African or Northeast African sun. In addition, Adam and Eve were made from the dirt of the ground, which, truthfully, would be brown or dark in color. It is worth noting that in 2003, the people who currently inhabit the land of Israel had the second-highest rate of skin cancer in the world, particularly melanoma, a serious and potentially fatal form of skin cancer caused by prolonged exposure to the sun's ultraviolet rays.[65] This statistic raises important questions about the historical and genetic connections between the region's modern and original inhabitants, especially given the intense sun and harsh climate.

If the biblical Israelites lived for generations in regions of intense sunlight, their skin tones would have adapted to these conditions, rich in melanin for sun protection. Job declared, *"My skin is black upon me, and my bones are burned with heat" (Job 30:30, KJV).* Solomon wrote, *"I am black, but comely, O ye daughters of Jerusalem, as the tents of Kedar, as the curtains of Solomon" (Song of Solomon 1:5, KJV).*[66] These verses prompt deeper reflection on the historical representation and identity of the Israelites in Scripture.

---

[65] In 2003, Israel had the second-highest rate of skin cancer in the world, trailing only Australia. The incidence rate among Israeli Jews was significantly higher than among Arab Israelis, suggesting a connection to skin pigmentation and UV adaptation. See "Health in Israel," Wikipedia; Haaretz, "Israel's Skin Cancer Rate Second Highest in the World" (May 13, 2003); Israel Cancer Association reports.

[66] Song of Solomon 1:5 (KJV). The Hebrew word used here, shachor, means "black" or "dark." Kedar, named for Ishmael's second son, derives from the Hebrew qadar, meaning "dark" or "dusky." See Strong's Concordance, H7023 and H6938.

Building upon these scriptural references, we see further connections in context. Kedar was Ishmael's second son, named from the Hebrew *qadar*, meaning "dark," "dusky," or "powerful." The following verse states, *"Look not upon me, because I am swarthy, because the sun hath scorched me. My mother's sons were incensed against me; they made me keeper of the vineyards; but mine own vineyard have I not kept" (Song of Solomon 1:6, ASV).* The term "swarthy" in the dictionary denotes dark-skinned. Many skeptics attempt to downplay specific biblical references by arguing they don't pertain to skin color.

To deepen this understanding, consider human origins through both Scripture and genetics. Early humans needed the genetic capacity to develop diverse physical traits, enabling humanity to populate the Earth. Melanin, which determines skin color, is central. Populations with more melanin can produce the full range of skin tones, since lighter pigmentation results from recessive traits. In contrast, populations without melanin cannot naturally produce darker skin. This is seen in conditions like albinism, where lighter skin occurs but new pigmentation does not. Whether approached biblically or scientifically, it is crucial to recognize the role of genetics and melanin in human diversity.

Geography highlights that Africa and the so-called Middle East have intense heat and arid climates. Medical evidence shows that people with darker skin can experience increased darkening during extreme dehydration, malnutrition, or illness—even after death. These changes result directly from the body's response to water deprivation, sun exposure, and harsh conditions, aligning with biblical descriptions such as Lamentations 5:10, which depicts famine as darkening the Israelites' skin.[67]

In contrast to the effects experienced by those with darker skin, people with lighter skin tend to grow paler during illness or starvation. When exposed to intense sunlight, fair skin often reddens, becomes irritated, and is prone to long-term damage, including skin cancer and premature aging. This difference underscores melanin's protective role, not just in appearance but as a biological shield. Melanin-rich skin is adapted to thrive under intense UV radiation, which is common in regions where early civilizations developed. Sunlight is essential for sustaining life, agriculture, and health, and melanin would have been crucial for survival in sun-rich areas, the setting of much early biblical history. This is by God's design.

When discussing the people of the Bible and humanity's origins, we must consider melanin, climate, and genetic science. These factors affirm the plausibility of darker-skinned origins and challenge modern misinterpretations that disconnect Scripture from science and history. Because man was created in the image and likeness of God, we must ask: What is the image and likeness of God? The Scriptures provide us with an idea:

> *"As I looked, thrones were placed, and the Ancient of Days took his seat; his clothing was white as snow, and the hair of his head like pure wool; his throne was fiery flames; its wheels were burning fire" (Daniel 7:9–10, KJV).*

---

[67] Lamentations 5:10 (KJV): "Our skin was black like an oven because of the terrible famine." The Hebrew word kamar used here means "to grow hot" or "to become dark/blackened."

"The hairs of his head were white, like white wool, like snow. His eyes were like a flame of fire, his feet were like burnished bronze, refined in a furnace, and his voice was like the roar of many waters" (Revelation 1:14–15, KJV).

Interestingly, the original Greek text suggests a metal closer to copper rather than bronze, highlighting how subtle shifts in translation can affect our understanding of Scripture. These nuances remind us that every translation involves interpretive choices, and even small changes can influence how we perceive the imagery and meaning of God's Word.

"And he that sat was to look upon like a jasper and a sardine stone: and there was a rainbow round about the throne, in sight like unto an emerald" (Revelation 4:3, KJV).

Image 6: A picture of Jasper stones.

Image 7: Sardius stones, also known as sardine or carnelian stones.

Taking all this into account, both Jasper and Sardius are brownish-red. Regardless of whether other churches address this, understand that your dark skin is not what society has falsely portrayed. It is not sad, depressing, sinful, monstrous, or villainous. These negative labels are distortions. Dark skin is the origin of all other tones, reflecting dominant genetics, prestige, strength, and power. The term "human" (hue-man) itself refers to a "colored man."[68] This is the tone the Most-High chose as the foundation–the earth's tone, like a painter's canvas for humanity.

---

[68] The English word human derives from the Latin humanus, which is related to homo (man) and humus (earth or ground), reflecting the idea of mankind as "earthly beings." It is not etymologically derived from the English word "hue." See: The Oxford English Dictionary; Online Etymology Dictionary.

Image 8: A tomb painting from Gebelein.

Viewed through this lens, Joseph and Mary fled to Egypt to hide the Christ child from Herod. Moses and Paul, though both Hebrews, were mistaken for Egyptians, who descended from Ham's son Mizraim. Some contend that Europeans later damaged Egyptian statues' noses and lips to obscure their heritage. Scripture suggests the first human had a melanated complexion, and research by National Geographic indicates that Adam was brown-skinned.[69]

[69] Modern genetic and anthropological research indicates that early humans likely had dark skin, as higher levels of melanin would have been necessary for protection against intense ultraviolet radiation in equatorial regions where humanity is widely believed to have originated. While figures such as Adam are theological, not scientific, studies on early human populations support the likelihood of darker skin tones. See: National Geographic Society; Smithsonian Institution.

Image 9: The Sacrifice of Isaac from the Catacomb of Via Latina in Rome.

Many images found in the Catacombs of Rome depict biblical figures as melanated.[70] Some Russian Orthodox icons from the 15th and 16th centuries depict certain biblical figures with darker complexions, including deep brown tones, which some scholars and observers have interpreted as reflecting African or Afro-Asiatic features rather than the lighter European portrayals common in later Western art.[71] This

---

70 The Catacombs of Via Latina in Rome contain 4th-century frescoes depicting biblical scenes, including the Sacrifice of Isaac. Several of these images portray biblical figures with dark complexions, providing early artistic evidence of how the first Christians understood the ethnic appearance of scriptural characters. See Antonio Ferrua, The Unknown Catacomb: A Unique Discovery of Early Christian Art (New Lanark: Geddes & Grosset, 1991).

71 Oleg Tarasov notes that Russian iconography preserved a wide range of visual traditions influenced by Byzantine and Eastern Christian art. See Oleg Tarasov, *Icon and Devotion: Sacred Spaces in Imperial Russia* (London: Reaktion Books, 2002), 78–82. See also "The Many Faces and the Many Colors of Christ," *Public*

reveals that other nations are also aware of the truth but choose to conceal it to uphold a false narrative.

What Is God's Likeness?

> *"And God said, Let us make man in our image, after our likeness: and let them have dominion over the fish of the sea, and over the fowl of the air, and over the cattle, and over all the earth, and over every creeping thing that creepeth upon the earth" (Genesis 1:26, KJV).*

According to Strong's Concordance, the word "likeness" refers to resemblance, model, fashion, manner, or similitude.[72] It is similar to how a child reflects a parent's image. When you see the child, you see the parent's likeness. In the same way, when we look at Adam, we see a reflection of dominion. He walked and spoke with authority. Whatever Adam named a creature became its identity. His words carried power and definition.

> *"Now out of the ground the LORD God had formed every beast of the field and every bird of the heavens and brought them to the man to see what he would call them. And whatever the man called every living creature, that was its name" (Genesis 2:19, ESV).*

When God placed Adam in the Garden, He instructed him to "dress it and keep it." While this is often interpreted as a command to work, it

---

Orthodoxy, July 6, 2020, which discusses how Orthodox and Ethiopian icon traditions sometimes depicted Christ and biblical figures with darker skin tones.

[72] Strong's Concordance, H1823: demuwth (דמות), meaning "resemblance, likeness, model, shape." It conveys similarity or correspondence in form, nature, or character.

is important to understand that the type of labor we associate with work today did not begin until after the fall of Adam and Eve. In this context, "dress it and keep it" meant that Adam was tasked with maintaining, caring for, preserving, protecting, and exercising dominion over the Garden and its animals.

We are a people who feel, relate, and love. These are traits that reflect God's characteristics. Throughout the Scriptures, we witness God's love, compassion, understanding, disappointment, anger, jealousy, and acquaintance with grief and sorrow. We experience emotions as God does. We possess an innate morality that evokes these emotions within our humanity. We have intellect, conscience, reason, and a sense of right and wrong. Animals act on instinct; humans can choose between good and evil.

Humanity is composed of three parts: spirit, soul, and body. Each of us is a single person with these three distinct components. We are made in God's image, and He operates in three distinct functions: Father, Son, and Holy Spirit. Though interconnected and all one, the spirit, soul, and body are distinct and serve different functions. God is meant to rule in man's spirit; the spirit should govern the soul, and the soul should direct the body. The spirit receives God's will, the soul interprets it, and the body acts on it.

In considering these truths—scriptural references, genetic science, and the realities of climate—it becomes clear that the original human experience is deeply connected to melanin and divine design. Understanding who we are and where we come from is not only a matter of history or biology but also a spiritual reflection on our identity, purpose, and worth. Embracing this knowledge challenges distortion, restores dignity, and calls us to live out the full image and likeness of God, empowered by the heritage we inherit.

We create, like God, through our skills and abilities, the union of marriage and reproduction, natural gifts (such as playing the piano and singing), and our words.

> *"Death and life are in the power of the tongue: and they that love it shall eat the fruit thereof" (Proverbs 18:21, KJV).*

God is the ultimate Creator, and as His image-bearers, we are uniquely creative in art, music, language, innovation, and more. In addition, we rest daily from our labor, just as God rested from all His work on the seventh day. When God created man, He breathed His own breath into him, making God's essence the foundation of human existence. However, this image and likeness were distorted by an identity crisis. Since man has sinned, he is not as fully like God as he was before. His moral purity has been lost, and his character no longer reflects God's holiness. His intellect is corrupted by falsehood and misunderstanding; his speech no longer continually glorifies God, and his relationships are often governed by selfishness rather than love. Though man still has the image of God, various aspects of that image have been distorted or lost. This is why Christ came: to restore our nature to God's nature.

> *"I will praise thee; for I am fearfully and wonderfully made: marvellous are thy works; and that my soul knoweth right well" (Psalm 139:14, KJV).*[73]

---

[73] Psalm 139:14 (KJV). The Hebrew word translated "fearfully" (yare) implies reverence and awe, while "wonderfully" (palah) means to be distinctly made or set apart.

You are uniquely formed and made with distinction. Never allow the lies of the enemy to cause you to feel lost in your identity or that you do not measure up. You are God's greatest masterpiece! The image of the Most-High in human lives was not destroyed, but it was damaged by the Fall in Genesis, Chapter 3. We still bear the image and likeness of God, but sin distorts them, just as a broken mirror distorts an image. However, by accepting the Messiah and surrendering our lives to Him, we are transformed back into the image of the Most-High.

Because of this, it is vital that you know who you are. Who we think we are determines how we live out our lives. People who dislike themselves often engage in destructive behavior. They get into bad relationships. They disfigure or change their appearance. They damage friendships. They burn bridges. They cause more damage to their emotions, minds, and bodies. They can even cause breakdowns within themselves.

People who do not know who they are will conform to whatever image you present to them. This is why the systems around us work tirelessly to keep images in front of us. They know our identity has been distorted, damaged, and altered over time. So, they replace it with images that keep us in a state of downtrodden, destructive despair. They give us music that is destructive to our community, role models that are destructive to our community, narratives that normalize dysfunction, and platforms that reward broken behavior.

They celebrate what degrades us and silence what develops us. They magnify chaos and minimize character. Because if they can control what you see, they can influence how you think. And if they can influence how you think, they can shape how you live. So now you have people imitating images they were never designed to reflect, chasing identities they were never assigned, and living beneath a purpose they were born to walk in.

But the truth is, your identity was never supposed to come from what is in front of you; it was always meant to come from what is within you. And until you break away from the false images, you will keep reproducing a false version of yourself. Because whatever you consistently behold, you eventually become. That is why you must be intentional about what shapes your vision, because your vision will always determine your direction.

Not knowing who you are can lead you to rely on the wrong things, causing you to hurt over and over again instead of healing. However, when we understand who God created us to be, we discover an identity rooted in truth that offers us the purpose God wants us to fulfill. So, if you have been entertaining a negative self-image, letting other people define your identity, letting things that are not good for you determine your identity, or believing lies the enemy has brought you—I want to remind you that you are made in the image and likeness of God. This day, choose to believe what God says about you. Rise, my brother and my sister. Know who you are and whose you are!

CHAPTER THREE

The Seed

Ezekiel is a prophet of God who prophesied against the king of Tyre in Ezekiel 28:12–17.[74] Tyre was a Phoenician city located in what is now Lebanon. During the time of Ezekiel's prophecy, Ithobaal III was reigning as king, and Jerusalem was in a fallen state, conquered by the Babylonians. However, the city of Tyre took the fall of Jerusalem as an opportunity to strengthen its wealth and status. Ezekiel sees the king of Tyre as a metaphor for Lucifer and compares his pride to Lucifer's before his fall. God speaks through the Prophet Ezekiel to deliver a lamentation over the king of Tyre. The passage describes a being full of wisdom and perfect in beauty, who once dwelt in Eden and was adorned with every precious stone. This being was anointed and held a high, holy position, walking among the fiery stones of God's presence. Created perfectly, he later became corrupted by pride and sin. His heart was lifted because of his beauty, and his splendor spoiled his wisdom. As a result, God declared judgment, casting him down from the mountain of God to the ground, exposed before kings in shame.

These passages reveal that Lucifer was not only in Eden but specifically in the Garden of Eden, a place symbolic of paradise and

---

[74] Ezekiel 28:12–17 (KJV). The Prophet Ezekiel delivered this oracle against the king of Tyre around 586–573 BC. The historical king at this time was Ithobaal III, who reigned approximately 591–573 BC. Josephus records that Nebuchadnezzar besieged Tyre for thirteen years during Ithobaal's reign (Against Apion 1.21). Many scholars and theologians read Ezekiel's lamentation as a dual reference—addressing both the historical king and, metaphorically, the fall of Lucifer. See Daniel I. Block, The Book of Ezekiel: Chapters 25–48, NICOT (Grand Rapids: Eerdmans, 1998).

of God's presence. His garments, adorned with precious stones, represent beauty, wealth, and a highly exalted status. Ezekiel also notes that the workmanship of musical instruments was prepared in him on the day Lucifer was created, suggesting that he may have possessed musical abilities used in the worship of God. And as a covering cherub, he held a high-ranking position, responsible for guarding God's throne. This prophecy highlights that Lucifer was a created being, endowed with free will, yet he allowed pride and corruption to take root. What was once holy and pure ultimately became defiled.

So, in Genesis Chapter 3, Lucifer, now Satan, who means "adversary", utilized the serpent to tempt Adam and Eve.

The War Over the Seed Begins

> *"Now the serpent was more subtil than any beast of the field which the Lord God had made. And he said unto the woman, Yea, hath God said, Ye shall not eat of every tree of the garden?" (Genesis 3:1, KJV).*

How was Eve so comfortable speaking with the serpent? The apocryphal Book of Jubilees shows that all the animals spoke one language. This one language was the original language of Hebrew, also known as the tongue of creation.[75]

> *"And on that day was closed the mouth of all beasts, and of cattle, and of birds, and of whatever walketh, and of*

---

[75] The Book of Jubilees presents the idea that Hebrew was the original language given to humanity. In Jubilees 12:25–27, it states that Hebrew was preserved and taught to Abraham after being lost among the nations following the Tower of Babel, suggesting it as the foundational or "holy" language associated with creation.

whatever moveth, so that they could no longer speak: for they had all spoken one with another with one lip and with one tongue" (Jubilees 3:28).[76]

Look further at Jubilees 12:26:

"And I opened his mouth, and his ears and his lips, and I began to speak with him in Hebrew in the tongue of the creation" (Jubilees 12:26)

After the fall of Adam and Eve, the Most-High caused all animals to cease speaking. The only recorded instance of an animal speaking again appears in Numbers 22:28, when Balaam was riding his donkey.[77] As Balaam journeyed to meet Balak, king of Moab, the angel of the Most-High stood in the path to oppose him. Though Balaam could not see the angel, his donkey could and turned aside multiple times to avoid the divine presence. Frustrated, Balaam struck the donkey, prompting the Most-High to open the donkey's mouth. The animal spoke, asking why Balaam had beaten her, and then the Most-High opened Balaam's eyes so that he, too, could see the angel. This miraculous event served as both a warning and a rebuke, showing that God can use even the unexpected to convey His will and prevent a man from going astray.

---

[76] *Jubilees* 3:28 states that after Adam and Eve were expelled from the Garden of Eden, Adam offered incense consisting of frankincense, galbanum, stacte, and sweet spices in an act of worship and repentance before God. This passage reflects Second Temple Hebrew tradition concerning the aftermath of humanity's fall and is not recorded in the canonical text of Genesis.

[77] Numbers 22:28–31 (KJV). The account of Balaam's donkey speaking is one of two instances in Scripture where an animal is given the power of speech (the other being the serpent in Genesis 3).

So, in Genesis 3:2–7, Eve, in the Garden of Eden, is approached by the serpent, who questions God's command not to eat from the Tree of Knowledge. Eve explains that God forbade them to eat or even touch the tree, warning that they would die if they did. The serpent deceives her, claiming they would not surely die but instead would become like God, knowing good and evil. Persuaded by the serpent's argument, Eve sees the tree as desirable for gaining wisdom, so she eats the fruit and gives some to Adam, who also eats. As a result, their eyes are opened, and they realize they are naked. Feeling ashamed, they sew fig leaves together to cover themselves. This moment marks the beginning of humanity's disobedience to God and the entrance of sin into the world.

According to *The Legends of the Jews* by Louis Ginzberg, it was believed that the fig was the forbidden fruit, which is why they were able to take those fig leaves and sew them together to make a covering.[78] Another reason to consider this view is that Yahshua cursed the fig tree in Mark 11. However, I have not found definitive biblical evidence for this idea.

> *"And the Lord God said unto the serpent, Because thou hast done this, thou art cursed above all cattle, and above every beast of the field; upon thy belly shalt thou go, and dust shalt thou eat all the days of thy life: And I will put enmity between thee and the woman, and between thy seed and her seed; it*

[78] Louis Ginzberg, The Legends of the Jews, trans. Henrietta Szold, 7 vols. (Philadelphia: Jewish Publication Society, 1909–1938), vol. 1, "The Fall of Man." Ginzberg records the Jewish tradition that the fig was the forbidden fruit, noting that "only the fig-tree granted him permission to take of its leaves. That was because the fig was the forbidden fruit itself."

shall bruise thy head, and thou shalt bruise his heel" (Genesis 3:14–15, KJV).[79]

Enmity means hostility, animosity, or even hatred. What makes this significant is that after Adam and Eve disobeyed God's command, the Most-High declared that He would place enmity between the serpent (representing the devil) and the woman, and between the serpent's seed and the woman's seed. This reveals that both the serpent and the woman have a "seed" (or offspring), but the prophecy specifically says that the woman's seed will bruise the head of the serpent, while the serpent will bruise His heel. This is a powerful prophecy: it foretells that the woman will bear a child, but notably, it does not mention the seed of a man. Biologically, "seed" is always associated with the man, not the woman. This is a clear indication of a supernatural birth—a child born without the involvement of a man's seed. God did not use the seed of a man to birth Christ because the Messiah needed to come into the world without inheriting the sin nature that all humanity carries from Adam.

According to Scripture in Romans 5:12, sin entered the human race through Adam. Every person born to human parents inherits both physical life and a spiritual nature corrupted by sin. If Yahshua had been conceived by the natural union of man and woman, He would have shared in that fallen nature, making Him unable to be the perfect, sinless sacrifice required to redeem humanity. Instead, God caused Mary to conceive by the power of the Holy Spirit, ensuring that Yahshua was fully human through His mother yet free from the

---

[79] Genesis 3:14–15 (KJV). This passage, known as the protoevangelium ("first gospel"), is widely regarded as the first messianic prophecy in Scripture. See Walter C. Kaiser Jr., The Messiah in the Old Testament (Grand Rapids: Zondervan, 1995), 37–42.

inherited corruption of Adam's line. He was also fully divine, carrying the very nature of God. This miraculous virgin birth fulfilled prophecy and safeguarded the purity of His bloodline, so He could truly be the "Lamb without blemish" who takes away the sin of the world.[80]

Moreover, just as it is common knowledge that if you want to kill a snake, you strike its head, this prophecy signaled a future fatal blow to the serpent, announced by the Most-High Himself. From that moment forward, the enemy understood that his ultimate defeat would come through a specific seed, a promised seed. So, his mission, then, has been to corrupt, delay, or destroy that seed.

Because only the Most-High is omniscient, omnipresent, and omnipotent, the enemy could not know the exact timing, person, or method by which the seed would come. He could not predict the "when," "where," "who," or "how." What is important to highlight, however, is that the devil understood the weight of God's words. He knew this seed would be born through a supernatural act of God. And because of that, he has made ongoing attempts to corrupt the timeline of events—trying to prevent what he knew would bring about his ultimate defeat. Let us briefly consider what unfolded in this effort throughout history.

One of the earliest attacks on the promised seed occurred when Adam and Eve's son Cain killed his brother Abel. Abel carried the lineage through which Christ would eventually come. Cain's act was

---

80 The virgin birth of Christ fulfills the prophecy in Isaiah 7:14 and is recorded in Matthew 1:22–23. It affirms both His divine origin and sinless nature, qualifying Him as the spotless sacrifice. The description "Lamb without blemish" is drawn from First Epistle of Peter 1:18–19, while Gospel of John 1:29 identifies Christ as "the Lamb of God, which taketh away the sin of the world."

influenced by the adversary, who attempted to destroy the seed. In Genesis 6, fallen angels corrupted humanity by taking human women as wives, producing hybrid offspring. This led to widespread seed corruption, the distortion of nature, and an increase in demonic activity.[81] Throughout the Old Testament, Baal became a prominent false god. One of the primary ways Baal was worshiped was through child sacrifice, a direct influence of Satan intended to wipe out the seed. In Exodus, Pharaoh ordered all Hebrew baby boys to be killed. This was another attempt to eliminate the seed and prevent the fulfillment of God's promise. During the time of Christ's birth, King Herod commanded that all male children two years old and under be killed. His goal was to stop the arrival of the prophesied Messiah and intercept biblical prophecy. When Christ was crucified, the enemy believed he had won. This event represented the bruising of the seed's heel. But when Christ rose from the dead, it became clear that this was the striking of the serpent's head—the fulfillment of the prophecy and the ultimate victory over the enemy.

So, once Adam and Eve fell, God had to restore order. In response to Adam and Eve's disobedience, the Most-High begins by addressing each party involved in the fall, bringing consequences that align with the roles He had given them. To the woman, He declares that her pain in childbirth will greatly increase, and her relationship with her husband will be marked by tension; her desire for him will be coupled with his authority over her. This pronouncement reshapes the

[81] Luke 1:35 (KJV): "The Holy Ghost shall come upon thee, and the power of the Highest shall overshadow thee: therefore also that holy thing which shall be born of thee shall be called the Son of God."

dynamic between man and woman, introducing struggle where harmony once existed.

Then God turns to Adam, holding him accountable for having listened to his wife rather than obeying His direct command. The ground, once freely fruitful, is now cursed, and Adam will have to labor with sweat and toil to produce food. Thorns and thistles will now resist his efforts, a constant reminder of the cost of sin. Life will become a struggle for survival, and eventually, the man will return to the dust from which he came—death entering as the final enemy in the human experience.

Yet in His mercy, God clothed Adam and Eve with garments of skin, showing that even in judgment, He provides for their needs and covers their shame. Yet, because they had eaten from the tree of the knowledge of good and evil, God could not allow them to take from the tree of life and live forever in a fallen state. So, He drove them out of the Garden of Eden and placed a cherub with a flaming sword to guard the way to the tree of life. What was once a place of perfect fellowship was now closed to them, but God's act preserved the promise of redemption that would one day restore access to eternal life.

Why the Fall?

For creation to meet God's expectation, there must be testing. God tested man with obedience. God did not create us out of necessity, but out of a desire to love. As love itself, He gave us free will—the ability to choose or reject Him. Though He knew sin could enter through this freedom, He still chose to give it because love is most meaningful when freely chosen. Our love and appreciation for God are shown through our obedience. Because of that, Satan's goal is to cause humanity to walk according to his actions, and that is to rebel. The spirit of rebellion has been running rampant throughout this world for ages. Rebellion is rooted in pride, stubbornness, and self-centeredness. It creates an opening for the enemy to bring destruction into our lives, distorting our understanding of truth and placing us in opposition to God.

In the First Book of Adam and Eve, the devil explains to Adam that his hostility, envy, and sorrow are because of Adam. Lucifer was expelled from glory because God created Adam in His image and commanded all angels to reverence Adam. Michael led the act of homage, but Lucifer refused, claiming he was created before Adam and should be worshiped instead. In response to this defiance, God became wrathful and banished Lucifer and his angels to earth. Lucifer, grieving over Adam's joy, deceived Adam's wife, causing Adam's expulsion from paradise, mirroring Lucifer's own fall from glory.[82]

What is significant about the seed is that it is important for the production of life. From the seed, life is produced, but not just produced: from the seed, life begins, builds, and becomes. Abel was probably thought to be the carrier of the promised "seed" as foretold in Genesis 3:15—the one who would crush the serpent's head and reverse the curse of sin.[83] But that hope was violently shattered when

---

[82] The First Book of Adam and Eve (also called The Conflict of Adam and Eve with Satan), Chapters 12–16. This is a pseudepigraphal text dating to approximately the 5th–6th century AD. See S. C. Malan, trans. The Book of Adam and Eve, Also Called the Conflict of Adam and Eve with Satan (London: Williams and Norgate, 1882).
[83] Genesis 3:15 (KJV): "And I will put enmity between thee and the woman, and between thy seed and her seed; it shall bruise thy head, and thou shalt bruise his heel."

Cain, their firstborn, murdered his younger brother. With Abel dead and Cain disqualified by his sin, the promise seemed in jeopardy. Yet God was not finished. When their third son, Seth, was born, hope was once again restored. He may not have been the Messiah himself, but he could carry the righteous bloodline through which the Savior would come. Look at what Eve stated in Genesis 4:25. She declared, *"God has appointed me another seed instead of Abel, whom Cain slew."*[84] In this statement, she acknowledged that God's redemptive plan was still in motion and that the lineage of the Messiah would continue through Seth. But that did not stop the enemy from trying to disrupt the plan—human hearts and actions were becoming increasingly corrupt. In Genesis Chapter 6, things became so corrupt on the earth that God determined to wipe out man and beast with a flood. Because God's Word cannot be voided, the seed still needed to be preserved. This became the purpose of Noah's Ark. The Ark was actually God's means of preserving the "seed."

The enemy understood that his defeat would come through a promised seed, so his objective became to corrupt or even destroy it. However, remember that only the Most-High is ever-present, all-knowing, and all-powerful qualities that the devil does not possess. As a result, Satan could not predict the exact time, place, person, or method through which the seed would come, so he attempted to cover all possibilities. Because he knew the nature and truth of the Most-High, he recognized exactly what the prophecy foretold. He understood that his downfall would occur through a virgin birth, so he set out to counterfeit and distort the prophecy, creating false

[84] Genesis 4:25 (KJV).

narratives to divert humanity's attention from the true promise. This deceptive strategy began all the way back in Babylon, with three key figures: Nimrod, Semiramis, and her son Tammuz.

Nimrod is one of the Bible's most mysterious figures, described as a *"mighty hunter before the Lord"* and a powerful ruler whose kingdom encompassed cities such as Babylon and Nineveh.[85] His power came through military strength and conquest. Because of his connection to Babylon—a symbol of rebellion against God in books like Daniel and Revelation—Nimrod is often seen as representing opposition to divine authority. The Prophet Micah, in Chapter 5:6, even refers to the "land of Nimrod," linking him to Babylon and Assyria, which were later enemies of Israel.[86]

Though the Bible does not directly say he led the rebellion, later traditions connect Nimrod to the building of the Tower of Babel in Genesis 11, a symbol of human pride and defiance against God. The Hebrew historian Josephus expands on this tradition in *Antiquities of the Jews*, portraying Nimrod as a tyrant who promoted false religion and resisted God's rule.[87] His legacy is that of a powerful kingdom builder who ultimately stood against the Most-High, serving

---

85 Genesis 10:8–12. Nimrod is described as "a mighty hunter before the LORD" whose kingdom included Babel, Erech, Accad, and Calneh in the land of Shinar, and later Nineveh and other cities in Assyria. The Hebrew historian Josephus expands on Nimrod's character in *Antiquities of the Jews*, 1.4, portraying him as a tyrant who promoted rebellion against God. See also Alexander Hislop, The Two Babylons (Edinburgh: James Wood, 1858)—though scholars debate Hislop's historical methodology.

86 Micah 5:6 (KJV): And they shall waste the land of Assyria with the sword, and the land of Nimrod in the entrances thereof: thus shall he deliver us from the Assyrian, when he cometh into our land, and when he treadeth within our borders.

87 Josephus, *Antiquities of the Jews*, 1.4.2. Josephus writes that Nimrod "persuaded them not to ascribe it to God" and "gradually changed the government into tyranny." See William Whiston, trans. The Works of Josephus (Peabody, MA: Hendrickson, 1987).

as a warning about pride, ambition, and the use of power in rebellion against God.

Though not mentioned in the Bible, Semiramis (according to later traditions, Nimrod's wife and Queen of Babylon) appears in the writings of Eusebius and other ancient historians.[88] She is often associated with Sammur-amat, an Assyrian queen regent (811–806 BC). Some legends call Nimrod "Ninus," connecting them to Nineveh and Babylon, and claim he was killed and dismembered by Shem. Similar myths appear in Egyptian mythology, where Osiris's missing body part is linked to the obelisk.[89] After Nimrod's death, Semiramis supposedly claimed a supernatural pregnancy by Nimrod's spirit, promoting a false "virgin birth" that distorted the prophecy of Genesis 3:15.

To legitimize her rule, Semiramis claimed divine conception, saying the deceased Nimrod had ascended to the sun and impregnated her through its rays. She declared Nimrod the sun-god (Ba'al) and herself the moon goddess, presenting their son as a divine child. Semiramis further claimed to have been born from a "moon egg" that fell into the Euphrates, reinforcing her deity status. This myth later linked her to

---

[88] Semiramis is not mentioned in the canonical Scriptures. She appears in later traditions, including the writings of Eusebius of Caesarea (Chronicon) and Diodorus Siculus (Library of History, Book 2). The identification of Semiramis with the Assyrian queen regent Sammur-amat (811–806 BC) is debated among scholars, though the connection to Nimrod is drawn primarily from extrabiblical tradition. See Alexander Hislop, The Two Babylons (1858); for a critical assessment, see Ralph Woodrow, The Babylon Connection? (Palm Springs, CA: Ralph Woodrow Evangelistic Association, 1997).

[89] See Tim Gihring, "Ancient Egypt and the Mystery of the Missing Phallus," Minneapolis Institute of Art, December 12, 2018. The article discusses the Egyptian myth of Osiris's dismemberment, the loss of his phallus, and later symbolic and religious interpretations linked to Egyptian fertility imagery and ritual practices.

Ishtar (Easter), Eostre, and symbols of fertility such as the egg and rabbit.

Semiramis then gave birth to a son, known by various names across cultures: Damu (Sumerian), Dammuzi (Babylonian), Tammuz (Hebrew), and Adonis (Greek). After Tammuz's death, she claimed he ascended to the sun, completing what she called a "perfect union"-the devil's counterfeit of the divine Trinity: Nimrod as the father-god, Semiramis as the mother-goddess, and Tammuz as the divine son.

This triad was later reflected in various cultures: El, Bacchus, and Astarte among the Phoenicians; Ninus, Hercules, and Beltis among the Assyrians; Zeus, Dionysus, and Aphrodite among the Greeks; Jupiter, Attis, and Cybele among the Romans; Ra, Osiris, and Isis among the Egyptians; Vishnu, Krishna, and Isi among the people of India; Gilgamesh, Dumuzi, and Inanna in Sumerian culture; and Baal, Tammuz, and Ashtoreth among the Canaanites. Together, these three figures became the foundation of a Babylonian religion that spread far and wide. Deeply immoral and detestable practices marked their worship. These rites often included the use of fire, representing the sun as the giver of light. In this belief system, the deified Nimrod was revered as a bringer of enlightenment, one who gave humanity the knowledge to discern good from evil. This presents a strong connection to Lucifer, whose name means "light bearer."

> *"And no wonder, for even Satan disguises himself as an angel of light" (2 Corinthians 11:14, ESV).*

Semiramis, later worshiped as the Queen of Heaven, became central to Babylonian idolatry after Nimrod.

In this system, Nimrod symbolized the sun and Semiramis the moon, helping shape the worship of the sun, moon, and stars and the rise of astrology and the Zodiac. The mother-and-child image (Semiramis and Tammuz) spread across cultures as Isis and Horus in Egypt, Aphrodite and Eros in Greece, and Venus and Cupid in Rome. Over time, this Babylonian religion expanded worldwide, marked by secret rites, ritual cleansing, priestly absolution, holy water, and offerings to the Queen of Heaven. It also included temple prostitution and a forty-day mourning period for Tammuz (also known as Lent) before the festival of Ishtar, who was believed to restore him to life. In Scripture, the worship of Tammuz is condemned as part of Israel's idolatry.[90]

> *"Then he brought me to the entrance of the north gate of the house of the Lord, and behold, there sat women weeping for Tammuz" (Ezekiel 8:14, ESV).*

According to tradition, Tammuz was killed by a wild boar and later revived, symbolizing death and rebirth. The egg represented resurrection, while the evergreen tree honored his eternal nature and birth near the winter solstice, the "rebirth of the sun." During these rites, a boar's head was eaten and a Yule log burned. Tammuz, seen as the reincarnated sun god Nimrod, was celebrated on December 25th. Another important emblem was the sign of the cross, originally a symbol of life and fertility and possibly the first letter of Tammuz's

---

[90] Tammuz was a Mesopotamian fertility deity associated with death and seasonal rebirth rituals. Ancient mourning ceremonies connected to Tammuz involved lamentation practices that some historians link to later pagan fertility traditions surrounding Ishtar (Inanna). Scripture explicitly condemns this worship, as Ezekiel saw women "weeping for Tammuz" at the Temple in Jerusalem, identifying it as part of Israel's idolatry and spiritual corruption (Ezekiel 8:14). Some writers, most notably Alexander Hislop in *The Two Babylons*, have argued that later traditions such as Lent were influenced by ancient mourning rituals connected to Tammuz.

name in ancient script. This cross-like figure adorned altars and temples across Mesopotamia and surrounding regions long before it was ever associated with Christianity. There are even hieroglyphs with the symbol of the cross or the ankh in ancient Egypt, which would explain why they would later crucify Christ on a pagan symbol.

As the Roman Empire adopted Christianity under Emperor Constantine, there was a significant merging of pagan and Christian traditions.[91] Many pagan holidays were rebranded as Christian observances, transforming what were once "holy days" into "holidays" with mixed origins. This blending allowed formerly pagan customs to continue under the guise of Christianity, giving rise to traditions that seemed sacred or wholesome but were rooted in earlier, often idolatrous practices.

One such example is the fourth Sunday in Lent, originally associated with the mourning for Tammuz—a ritual period of lamentation for his death. Over time, this day evolved into what became known as Mothering Sunday in Europe. While it eventually became a day to honor earthly mothers with gifts and "mothering cakes," it also began to symbolize reverence for the "Mother Church." This transformation illustrates how ancient rituals, particularly those tied to the worship of false gods, were gradually absorbed and reframed within Christian contexts.

---

[91] Emperor Constantine convened the Council of Nicaea in 325 AD and issued the Edict of Milan in 313 AD, which granted religious tolerance throughout the Roman Empire. The merging of pagan and Christian customs under subsequent emperors is documented extensively. See Ramsay MacMullen, Christianity and Paganism in the Fourth to Eighth Centuries (New Haven: Yale University Press, 1997).

"The children gather wood, the fathers kindle fire, and the women knead dough, to make cakes for the queen of heaven. And they pour out drink offerings to other gods, to provoke me to anger" (Jeremiah 7:18, ESV).[92]

Mother's Day, which always falls on the second Sunday in May, and Father's Day, observed on the third Sunday in June, are part of a broader pattern of modern holidays that can be traced back to ancient pagan sun-worship traditions. These celebrations typically fall on a Sunday—the day named in honor of the sun itself, which was revered by many ancient cultures as the supreme deity, the source of light, life, and power.

In sun-worshiping systems, such as those of Babylon, Egypt, and Rome, the sun god held the highest place among the pantheon of deities.[93] By aligning celebrations with Sunday, these traditions subtly honored the sun god, even when later cloaked in cultural or religious reform. As Christianity spread and absorbed various cultural practices, many pagan-rooted observances were repurposed to take on new meanings, while often retaining their original timing and symbolism.

---

[92] Jeremiah 7:18 (ESV). The "Queen of Heaven" is generally identified with the Mesopotamian goddess Ishtar (Babylonian) or Astarte (Canaanite). See Susan Ackerman, Under Every Green Tree: Popular Religion in Sixth-Century Judah (Atlanta: Scholars Press, 1992).

[93] Ancient Near Eastern and Mediterranean religions often featured solar deities of great importance. In Mesopotamia, the sun god Shamash was associated with justice; in Egypt, Ra was a central figure in the state religion; and in Rome, Sol (later Sol Invictus) was honored in imperial worship. While the prominence of solar worship varied across cultures and periods, the sun frequently held a significant place within these religious systems. See: The Ancient Near East; The Oxford History of Ancient Egypt; Religions of Rome.

Now it becomes clear why many religions share similar elements—the enemy has long sought to confuse humanity about the true identity of the Messiah. Many belief systems present distorted versions of truth, often including the worship of multiple gods or even female deities. In contrast, biblical Christianity is firmly monotheistic, centered on the worship of one true God alone. Worship belongs solely to the Most-High, not to figures like Mary, whose veneration in some traditions is often viewed as influenced by earlier pagan practices. While polytheistic religions embrace many gods tied to different aspects of life, biblical faith upholds one eternal, all-powerful, and all-knowing God who alone is worthy of worship. Any form of worship involving multiple deities or elevating others to divine status falls under polytheism and paganism, which stand in contrast to the clear teachings of Scripture. So, the original prophecy of Genesis 3:15 became distorted through the pagan worship and religion of Nimrod, Semiramis, and Tammuz throughout history.

Going back to Genesis, the seed of Seth, or the lineage of Seth, ultimately became the vehicle through which Christ was born from an uncorrupted seed.

> *"And Adam knew his wife again; and she bare a son, and called his name Seth: For God, said she, hath appointed me another seed instead of Abel, whom Cain slew. And to Seth, to him also there was born a son; and he called his name Enos: then began men to call upon the name of the Lord" (Genesis 4:25–26, KJV).*

Satan understood that his ultimate defeat would come through the seed of the woman, as prophesied in Genesis 3:15, that this seed would one day crush his head. In response, his strategy became clear: corrupt the bloodline through which this promised seed would come. If he could taint or alter the lineage, he believed he could prevent the prophecy from being fulfilled. Even though Adam and Eve had fallen, God still chose to use mankind, the very beings created in His image, to bring about redemption. Why? Because, according to spiritual laws, mankind has legal authority on the earth. God works through people, and Satan knows this. Therefore, the enemy's plan was not just to lead humanity into sin, but to genetically corrupt humanity itself. This agenda became especially evident in Genesis 6, where we see fallen angels (the "sons of God") coming down and taking human women as wives, producing hybrid offspring known as the Nephilim.

This was not just about moral corruption; it was about genetic manipulation. The goal was not just to influence human behavior, but to pollute the human DNA so thoroughly that the pure bloodline through which the Messiah would come could no longer exist. Everything that makes you who you are (your identity, biology, and potential) is stored in your DNA.[94] That's your blueprint and your code. Satan's attack, both in ancient times and even now, aims to disrupt and alter that code. He isn't just after your soul—he's after your seed, your genetic integrity, and the continuation of God's divine image in humanity.

> *"And it came to pass, when men began to multiply on the face of the earth, and daughters were born unto them, that the*

---

94 Deoxyribonucleic acid (DNA) contains the genetic instructions used in the growth, development, functioning, and reproduction of living organisms. It serves as the biological blueprint that carries hereditary information, influencing physical traits and certain aspects of potential. See: National Human Genome Research Institute; National Library of Medicine.

sons of God saw the daughters of men that they were fair; and they took them wives of all which they chose" (Genesis 6:1–2, KJV).

The angels understood the sacred purpose of marriage and its divine institution on earth. Marriage was designed by God to populate the earth and to preserve the purity of the human bloodline, protecting it from corruption through unnatural unions—such as those involving demonic or fallen angelic beings. This is why marriage is under such intense spiritual attack today: the enemy seeks to distort and destroy what God established to uphold His order.

The Hebrew word Nephilim means "the fallen ones."[95] These beings were the result of fallen angels (known as Watchers) who were originally assigned to watch over the earth. This particular chapter in Genesis has been widely debated and interpreted in different ways. However, two main interpretations are most commonly discussed.

The first view: the "Sons of God" are the sons of Seth. This view suggests that the godly descendants of Seth (Adam and Eve's third son) intermarried with the ungodly descendants of Cain. In this interpretation, "sons of God" refers to human lineage—those who followed the faith of Abel and Seth.

The second view: the "Sons of God" are angels. This view, supported by ancient texts like the Book of Enoch, claims that angelic beings descended to earth and sinned by taking human wives.[96]

---

95 The Hebrew word Nephilim (נפלים) derives from the root naphal, meaning "to fall." It has been variously translated as "giants," "fallen ones," or "mighty ones." See Michael S. Heiser, The Unseen Realm (Bellingham, WA: Lexham Press, 2015), 94–109.

96 1 Enoch 6:1–6. The Book of Enoch (also called 1 Enoch) is an ancient Jewish apocalyptic text dating to approximately the 3rd–1st centuries BC. It was preserved

However, their corruption extended beyond women. Enoch claims they also defiled "birds, beasts, and all flesh." Some interpretations suggest that this widespread corruption of nature could have resulted in the creation of unnatural hybrid creatures. From this perspective, I believe that just as the union of these fallen angels with human women produced giants (often called Nephilim), their interaction with animals might have produced massive and unusual creatures, possibly even what we now call dinosaurs. These beings would not have been part of God's original creation but instead a distorted imitation, creatures not designed by the Most-High, but rather manipulated by Satan and his angels as a counterfeit version of divine creation.

So, when the Bible speaks of the Sons of God committing these acts, which interpretation is correct? The phrase "sons of God" appears about four to five times in the Old Testament, and in each case, it refers to angelic beings, not humans. For example: *"The sons of God came to present themselves before the LORD, and Satan came also among them" (Job 1:6 and 2:1).*[97] *And: "When the morning stars sang together, and all the sons of God shouted for joy?" (Job 38:7).*[98] Clearly, these are spiritual beings, not descendants of Seth.

In Daniel 3, when the king of Babylon looked into the fiery furnace, he saw four men, not three. He described the fourth as looking like "a son of God" (in Aramaic), implying an angelic or divine being rather

---

in the Ethiopian Orthodox canon and in fragments among the Dead Sea Scrolls at Qumran. See George W. E. Nickelsburg, 1 Enoch 1: A Commentary on the Book of 1 Enoch, Chapters 1–36, 81–108, Hermeneia (Minneapolis: Fortress Press, 2001).

[97] Job 1:6 and 2:1 (KJV). The phrase "sons of God" (Hebrew: bene ha'elohim) in these passages refers to angelic beings presenting themselves before the Lord.

[98] Job 38:7 (KJV).

than a human, especially since the Messiah had not yet come in the flesh.[99] So, we conclude that the term "sons of God" consistently refers to angels throughout Scripture. Although God is often described as having a fatherly relationship with humanity, no one in the Old Testament is ever called the Son of God. That title is reserved for Christ alone.

In 2 Peter Chapter 2, the apostle speaks of the judgment coming upon the wicked and directly connects it to what happened in the days of Noah. He says that God did not spare the angels who sinned, nor the wicked cities of Sodom and Gomorrah.[100] Jude 1:6–7 also links these angels to sexual sin and perversion:

> *"And the angels which kept not their first estate, but left their own habitation, he hath reserved in everlasting chains under darkness unto the judgment of the great day. Even as Sodom and Gomorrah, giving themselves over to fornication, and going after strange flesh" (Jude 1:6–7, KJV).*

This strongly suggests that fallen angels engaged in immoral acts, similar to the sexual sin of Sodom. Some argue that angels cannot marry or have sexual relations based on the words of Christ in Scripture.

---

99 Daniel 3:25 (KJV). King Nebuchadnezzar saw a fourth figure in the fiery furnace whose appearance was "like the Son of God" (Aramaic: bar elahin). Most scholars understand this as a reference to an angelic being.

100 Second Epistle of Peter 2:4–6 (KJV) connects divine judgment across multiple events, stating that God "spared not the angels that sinned," and also brought judgment upon the ancient world in the days of Noah, as well as upon Sodom and Gomorrah, setting them forth as examples of consequences for wickedness.

"For in the resurrection they neither marry nor are given in marriage, but are like angels in heaven" (Matthew 22:30, ESV).[101]

The key phrase is "in heaven." In Matthew 22:30, Christ said angels in heaven do not marry, referring to their heavenly state. This does not address angels who left their proper domain, as described in Jude and in Genesis 6. Those angels took human form and interacted physically with women, producing the Nephilim—giants and mighty men whose corruption filled the earth and threatened the lineage that would bring forth the Messiah.

How Could They Do This?

Angels are spiritual beings, but they can interact with and manipulate the physical world; this ability is known as corporeality.[102] Across centuries, artists have often portrayed angels as physical, human-like beings, reflecting the belief that they could take on tangible form. This idea is supported in Scripture:

"Do not neglect to show hospitality to strangers, for thereby some have entertained angels unawares" (Hebrews 13:2, ESV).

---

[101] Matthew 22:30 (ESV); cf. Luke 20:35–36 (ESV). Christ's statement refers specifically to angels "in heaven"—not to fallen angels who abandoned their proper domain.

[102] Scripture presents angels as spiritual beings (Epistle to the Hebrews 1:14), yet also records instances in which they take on visible form and interact with the physical world, such as appearing to Abraham (Genesis 18:1–8) and Lot (Genesis 19:1–3). The term "corporeal" in this context is a theological description of their temporary physical manifestation, rather than implying a permanent physical body.

For example, in Genesis Chapter 19, the two angels who visited Lot in Sodom appeared as men and were physically able to eat, walk, and even escort Lot and his family out of the city before its destruction. So, these fallen angels left their heavenly abode, came down to earth, mated with human women, and produced giants.

> *"There were giants in the earth in those days; and also after that, when the sons of God came in unto the daughters of men, and they bare children to them, the same became mighty men which were of old, men of renown" (Genesis 6:4, KJV).*

The term "giants" is translated from the Hebrew word Nephilim, which can also mean "tyrant," "fallen ones," or "superhuman beings." These were not ordinary men; they were hybrids: part human, part angelic. They exhibited unnatural traits: extraordinary size, strength, deformities, and even spiritual corruption. The real problem here was the mixing of species, a direct violation of God's established order. In Genesis 1:24, God commanded every creature to reproduce "according to its kind." What happened in Genesis Chapter 6 was a perversion of this divine order—angels crossing a boundary that God never intended to be crossed. The resulting Nephilim were abominations, not part of God's original creation design.

The seed is important to the life that is within. This is why it is important to know whom you are becoming one with, because planting a seed in the wrong soil can produce stunted growth, unhealthy fruit, or even complete failure, reminding us that environment matters as much as intention. It is also important to note that a seed being planted into something outside of God's design will produce evil, whether naturally or spiritually. So, regarding the actions of the fallen angels, the Book of Enoch—a work excluded from the biblical canon but preserved in fragments among the Dead Sea Scrolls at Qumran —gives us greater detail.

In 1 Enoch 6:1–6, as humanity multiplied and beautiful daughters were born, a group of two hundred angels (called the sons of God) saw these women and desired them. Led by an angel named Semjâzâ, they decided to take human wives and have children with them. Fearing he would bear the guilt alone, Semjâzâ convinced the others to swear a binding oath to follow through together. They descended to earth during the days of Jared, Enoch's father, landing on Mount Hermon, which they named after the oath they swore there.

Image 10: Mount Hermon is the snowcapped ridge on the Lebanon-Syria border west of Damascus.

In 1 Enoch 7:1–5, the angels took human wives, had relations with them, and taught humanity forbidden knowledge, including magic, enchantments, and the use of plants and roots. Their wives became pregnant and gave birth to enormous giants, beings of immense size who devoured human food supplies.

When resources ran out, the giants turned violent, consuming humans and even preying on animals and each other, committing acts of bloodshed and corruption across the earth.

Historical accounts and ancient legends suggest that giants once roamed the earth. Revered for their immense size and perceived power, these beings were often worshiped as gods. Evidence of such reverence can be found in Egyptian history, as well as in the mythologies and records of many other ancient civilizations, including the Sumerians, Greeks, and Norse. Temples, statues, archaeological findings, and other writings point to a time when these towering figures played a central role in human culture and belief.

In 1 Enoch 8:1–2 and 10:1–5, the fallen angels corrupted humanity by teaching them forbidden knowledge. Azâzêl revealed how to forge weapons, craft armor, make jewelry, and use cosmetics and precious stones, leading people into vanity, violence, and immorality. Other angels taught sorcery, astrology, and the secrets of nature and the heavens, causing widespread corruption and sin on the earth.

As humanity's cries reached heaven, the Most-High responded. He sent the angel Uriel to warn Noah of the coming destruction through a great flood and instructed him to prepare for survival. God also commanded Raphael to bind Azâzêl hand and foot and cast him into a dark pit in the desert of Dûdaël, sealing him beneath jagged rocks so he could never see the light again.

Dûdaël in Hebrew means "kettle," "cauldron," or "pot," and El means "God" or "deity", literally translated as "the cauldron of God."[103] According to the Book of Enoch, Dûdaël is the designated place of imprisonment for Azazel, one of the chief fallen angels. Dûdaël (the Land of the Mighty Cauldrons) is traditionally identified as a rocky, uninhabited desert region, possibly east of Jerusalem. Due to its grim description, Dûdaël is often associated with the underworld and has been compared to Tartarus (in Greek mythology, a deep abyss used as a dungeon of torment) and Gehenna (a biblical term for a place of fiery judgment).

Josephus, the Hebrew historian, records in *Antiquities of the Jews*: *"For many angels of God accompanied with women, and begat sons that proved unjust, and despisers of all that was good, on account of the confidence they had in their own strength; for the tradition is, that these men did what resembled the acts of those whom the Grecians call giants."*[104]

The mixture of fallen angels and human women produced a different race, and unfortunately, that corrupted DNA remained in the earth. Goliath is one example—he was a giant, and he had four brothers who were giants as well. This is why David selected five stones when preparing to fight him. We also know there were giants in the land of Canaan when the Israelites went to spy out the land. The spies

---

[103] 1 Enoch 10:4–7. The name Dudael (or Dūda'ēl) is variously interpreted. Some scholars connect it to Beth Hadudo, a rocky terrain in the Judean desert associated with the scapegoat ritual in Leviticus 16. See James C. VanderKam and William Adler, eds. The Jewish Apocalyptic Heritage in Early Christianity (Assen: Van Gorcum, 1996).

[104] Josephus, *Antiquities of the Jews*, 1.3.1, records a tradition that angels cohabited with women and produced offspring described as powerful and corrupt, comparable to the "giants" of Greek tradition. This passage is often referenced in discussions of Genesis 6:1–4 and interpretations of the Nephilim.

described themselves as grasshoppers in comparison, emphasizing how massive these beings were. This suggests that what took place in Genesis Chapter 6 happened again after the flood. This is why God commanded the Israelites to cleanse the land. The offspring of these beings were still dwelling in Canaan—the very land God had promised to His people. The presence of giants like Og, king of Bashan, also confirmed that these beings persisted. Genesis 6:4 states that giants were on the earth "in those days, and also after that."[105]

> *"The Emims dwelt therein in times past, a people great, and many, and tall, as the Anakims; which also were accounted giants, as the Anakims; but the Moabites called them Emims" (Deuteronomy 2:10–12, KJV).*[106]

When we trace the Old Testament history of Israel, we find repeated references to giant clans that inhabited the land before and during Israel's conquest. These groups are collectively associated with the Rephaim (Rephaites), a broad term encompassing many ancient peoples of great size and strength. The Rephaim appear in Scripture as a general term for giant peoples. Deuteronomy 2:20 describes them as numerous and tall, feared by surrounding nations. Different regions knew them by different names. The Anakim, descended from Anak, were the most famous, and Numbers 13:33 links them to the Nephilim. The Emites lived in Moab and were as tall and mighty as the Anakim. The Horites were giant cave-dwellers in Seir until

[105] Genesis 6:4 states, "There were giants in the earth in those days; and also after that..." (KJV), indicating that the Nephilim or giant clans existed both before and after the Flood.

[106] Deuteronomy 2:10–12 (KJV). The Emites (Emim), Anakim, Horites, Zamzummites (Zamzummim), and Avvites are all described as giant peoples displaced by various nations. See also Numbers 13:33 and Deuteronomy 2:20–23.

displaced by Esau's descendants (the Edomites). The Zamzummites, another branch of the Rephaim, were later defeated by the Ammonites. The Avvites lived in Philistia until the Caphtorites from Crete destroyed them and became the Philistines. Though not giants themselves, the Philistines later sheltered surviving giant clans, such as those in Gath, including Goliath, carrying the giants' legacy into Israel's history and setting the stage for God's victories.

Because the seed was crucial to the birth of the Messiah, it had to remain pure—uncorrupted in blood, DNA, and soul. The Messiah had to come through a pure, untainted, and uncontaminated bloodline. This was essential for Him to be the perfect, sinless sacrifice for humanity. That is why He was born of a virgin, not conceived through the seed of a man, but by the power of the Holy Spirit. If Christ had come through natural human means, He would have inherited the sinful nature passed down from Adam. But by being supernaturally conceived, He bypassed the corrupted lineage of man, fulfilling prophecy and preserving the divine nature necessary to redeem the world.

Noah's lineage was not tainted or mixed with the evil that had spread through humanity. His genetic line remained undefiled. Although Noah was not without personal flaws, as shown by his drunken episode, his seed remained pure. From his three sons, Shem was chosen. Through Shem came Abraham, with whom God would establish His covenant. Abraham fathered Isaac, who then fathered Jacob, the father of the Children of Israel.

> *"But as the days of Noah were, so shall also the coming of the Son of man be. For as in the days that were before the*

flood they were eating and drinking, marrying and giving in marriage, until the day that Noe entered into the ark, and knew not until the flood came, and took them all away; so shall also the coming of the Son of man be" (Matthew 24:37–39, KJV).

What were they doing in Noah's day? And what are they doing now? They were corrupting animals—seen today through crossbreeding, cloning, and genetic modification. They were corrupting the ground—as seen today in cloning food, spraying chemicals, and genetically modifying crops. They were shedding innocent blood—seen today through acts like abortion, murder, and human trafficking. They were drinking blood, which is often symbolized or even displayed in modern media and music. They were mixing DNA—a reality in today's scientific experiments. They were creating new species, which is seen today as scientists push the limits of biology. They were living in a culture ruled by sexual immorality—sexual content is normalized and even celebrated in media, entertainment, and online platforms. They were engaging in blatant witchcraft. This is increasingly visible in mainstream entertainment. They normalized murder and violence, and a lack of conscience is becoming socially accepted.

But Noah found grace. I want you to know that now is not the time to let the enemy deceive you; now is not the time to be lulled into spiritual sleep; now is not the time to follow the crowd, but now is the time to stand for the truth. Just as Noah found grace in God's eyes, you can too. The prophecy of Genesis 3:15 was the first promise of a coming Savior, foretelling the ultimate defeat of Satan through the seed of the woman—fulfilled in Christ the Messiah.

The enemy has always been after the seed because he knows its power. His goal was and is to corrupt it, distort it, or destroy it entirely. Why? According to Genesis 3:15, the seed of the woman was prophesied to crush the serpent's head. That seed represents the plan of redemption, the lineage through which Christ, the Messiah, would come. Throughout history, we see Satan's consistent attempts to stop the seed. Every move was a desperate effort to prevent the arrival of the One who would overthrow him. Even today, the enemy still wages war against the seed, whether by attacking the next generation, undermining identity, or sowing lies into families and bloodlines, because he knows the truth: the seed carries the power of promise, purpose, and prophecy. And that seed, which was fulfilled in Christ, has already crushed his head at the cross, and now continues through the believers who carry the kingdom within them.

Just as light and darkness cannot coexist, neither can Heaven and Hell agree. There is no harmony between the enemy and the soul of the righteous. Holiness stands in direct opposition to evil. As long as we live in this world, there will be an ongoing conflict between the righteous and the wicked. This tension is not only external but also internal—where the flesh and the spirit wage war daily.

Those who are set apart for God must understand that the battle between good and evil is constant and that compromise is never an option for the righteous.

Why Is the Seed So Important?

The seed is important because it has power!

"Verily, verily, I say unto you, Except a corn of wheat fall into the ground and die, it abideth alone: but if it die, it bringeth forth much fruit" (John 12:24, KJV).

The seed holds within it the power to become something far greater than itself. Though it may appear small and insignificant, it is packed with extraordinary potential. Consider a towering tree—majestic and life-giving. It produces fruit, leaves, nutrients, and even oxygen. Yet all of that began with a single, tiny seed—something most would overlook or dismiss as unimportant. In the same way, you may seem small or insignificant to others, but you are filled with power when you are filled with the Spirit of the living God. As Scripture says in Acts 1:8, *"Ye shall receive power after that the Holy Ghost is come upon you."*[107]

Also, the seed is important because it has a purpose! Christ told a parable in Matthew 13:3–8 about a farmer who scattered seed. Some fell on the path and were eaten by birds, some on rocky ground and withered without roots, some among thorns that choked them, but some fell on good soil and produced an abundant harvest—thirty, sixty, or a hundredfold. When a seed is planted, it is done so with a clear purpose. It is meant to grow, to germinate, and to become something greater—to expand, multiply, and bear fruit. Your seed has this very purpose. The seed is never just a seed; it is a vessel of destiny and transformation. So, I encourage you to speak to your children and to the generations yet to come, and tell them that their seed has purpose. It will fulfill what God has called it to be. It will not die

---

[107] Acts 1:8 (KJV).

unaccomplished, unfulfilled, or unsuccessful. It carries a divine purpose that will be realized and released.

In addition to power and purpose, the seed is important because it also has promise! The promised Deliverer was not Abraham, who lied about Sarah, nor Moses, who disobeyed God, nor David, who sinned with another man's wife. No, the Deliverer was Christ the Messiah, not born from the seed of a man, uncorrupted by the devil's tactics, and unstained by sin or deceit. He came to redeem humanity, as Peter said, "with precious blood, like that of a lamb unblemished and spotless, the blood of Christ."[108] No one else could deal the blow to the head of the serpent. Christ alone is our Deliverer, the seed and the Savior who struck the serpent down when He died on the cross. The crown of thorns, the thirty-nine lashes, the nails in His hands, and the cross itself—all were the bruises on His heel. He suffered, bled, and died, but just like a seed, in death, life sprang forth. When a seed becomes a plant, it ceases to be just a seed. It loses its original identity and becomes something far greater, far better, and much stronger. Its very nature changes. The seed is important because it symbolizes hope for redemption and the eventual triumph over evil.

God chose a specific people through whom the promised seed would come. These are people created in the image and likeness of the Most-High. Yet, according to biblical history, they would go on to reject God, His prophets, the Messiah, and even the apostles. In doing so, they brought a curse upon themselves and their descendants. Their rebellion sparked a generational identity crisis—one that would echo

---

108 First Epistle of Peter 1:18–19 (KJV): "Forasmuch as ye know that ye were not redeemed with corruptible things... but with the precious blood of Christ, as of a lamb without blemish and without spot."

throughout the ages. But even in the midst of their fall, there remains hope: the saving power of the Most-High is still able to restore, reclaim, and redeem.

CHAPTER FOUR

The Sons

The story of Noah and his sons (Shem, Ham, and Japheth) is more than a tale of family relationships; it reveals God's unfolding plan for humanity after the flood. Their choices and descendants had a profound impact on the shaping of nations, history, and biblical prophecy. A vital truth that Black and Brown people need to understand is this: you are not adopted! For too long, many preachers have taught that we are merely adopted or grafted into God's family, largely because of uncertainty about the identity of the modern-day tribes of Israel. As a result, we have all been labeled as Gentiles. But to truly understand who the Gentiles were, and who they are today, we must return to the Book of Genesis, Chapter 10.

Among theologians, historians, and certain discussions, there exists a provocative theory: Noah may have been the first recorded case of albinism. While this idea may sound unusual at first, the passage cited in support of this theory is found in the Book of Enoch, a text attributed to Noah's great-grandfather and considered significant in some early Hebrew and Christian circles. In 1 Enoch 105:9–10, Lamech describes the unusual appearance of his newborn son, Noah:[109]

---

[109] 1 Enoch 105:9–10 and 105:1–3. The Book of Enoch (1 Enoch) is an ancient Jewish pseudepigraphal text preserved in the Ethiopian Orthodox canon and in fragments among the Dead Sea Scrolls. Lamech's description of Noah's unusual appearance has prompted speculation about albinism. See George W. E. Nickelsburg, 1 Enoch 1: A Commentary, Hermeneia (Minneapolis: Fortress Press, 2001).

"He answered and said, On account of a great event have I come to thee; and on account of a sight difficult to be comprehended have I approached thee—to my son Lamech a child has been born, who resembles not him; and whose nature is not like the nature of man. His colour is whiter than snow; he is redder than the rose; the hair of his head is whiter than white wool; his eyes are like the rays of the sun; and when he opened them he illuminated the whole house" (1 Enoch 105:9–10).

This vivid description has led some to speculate that Noah may have had albinism, a genetic condition characterized by a lack of melanin, resulting in very light skin, hair, and sensitivity to light—traits echoed in this passage. In 1 Enoch 105:1–3, Lamech expresses deep fear and confusion over his son's appearance:

"After a time, my son Mathusala took a wife for his son Lamech. She became pregnant by him, and brought forth a child, the flesh of which was as white as snow, and red as a rose; the hair of whose head was white like wool, and long; and whose eyes were beautiful. When he opened them, he illuminated all the house, like the sun—opening also his mouth, he spoke to the Lord of righteousness. Then Lamech his father was afraid of him; and flying away came to his own father Mathusala, and said, I have begotten a son unlike to other children. He is not human; but, resembling the offspring of the angels of heaven, is of a different nature from ours" (1 Enoch 105:1–3).

Here, Lamech does not just describe Noah as different; he believes the child might be angelic or otherworldly, resembling the Nephilim—the hybrid beings described earlier in the Book of Enoch and referenced in Genesis Chapter 6. The passage provides one of the few pre-flood descriptions of skin color and strongly implies that Noah's appearance was distinct from that of those around him, who were likely darker-skinned. Passages such as this, I believe, preserve perspectives that provide valuable background information.

The connection between Noah and albinism is more than literary. From a genetic standpoint, albinism appears significantly more frequently among Black populations in Africa than among white populations in Europe or North America.[110] Albinism rates in South Africa, for instance, are approximately 1 in 4,000—far higher than the worldwide average of 1 in 17,000 to 20,000. Among African Americans, the rate is approximately 1 in 10,000, compared to 1 in 36,000 among white Americans. Furthermore, a Black albino carries the full spectrum of melanin-related genetic material, meaning their children could be dark, medium, or light-skinned. In contrast, a Caucasian albino lacks the genetic diversity to produce children with dark skin.

If Noah were a person with albinism born into a dark-skinned lineage, he could still father children of varying skin tones. Therefore, it would be possible for Noah's son Japheth (progenitor of the Gentiles) to

---

[110] Albinism prevalence rates vary significantly by population. In sub-Saharan Africa, rates are notably higher: approximately 1 in 4,000 in South Africa and 1 in 1,400 in Tanzania, compared to approximately 1 in 17,000–20,000 worldwide and 1 in 36,000 among white Americans. Among African Americans, the rate is approximately 1 in 10,000. See Kromberg et al., "Albinism and Skin Cancer in Southern Africa," Clinical Genetics 36, no. 1 (1989): 43–52; Hong et al., "Albinism in Africa as a Public Health Issue," BMC Public Health 6, no. 212 (2006).

have been lighter-skinned as well. However, the reverse does not hold: a European albino cannot genetically produce dark-skinned offspring. This makes the argument statistically and genetically stronger for a Black or brown-skinned origin for Noah, rather than a European one.

Today, many Christians are quick to dismiss the Book of Enoch, often because it is not part of the traditional biblical canon. However, this dismissal is often based on tradition rather than personal study. What many do not realize is that Enoch is directly referenced and validated in the New Testament, particularly by Peter and Jude. In 2 Peter 2:4, Peter refers to fallen angels being cast into hell and held in chains—an event not detailed in the Old Testament Scriptures but elaborated upon in the book of Enoch.[111] Jude 1:6 echoes this. And Jude 1:14 goes even further, directly quoting from the Book of Enoch: *"And Enoch also, the seventh from Adam, prophesied of these, saying, Behold, the Lord cometh with ten thousands of his saints."*[112] In these passages, Enoch is called a prophet—a role not mentioned in Genesis, which states that he "walked with God." Jude's quotation confirms that the early church regarded Enoch as a legitimate prophetic source rather than a mythological figure.

If Noah were a dark-skinned albino, then he carried the genetic potential to repopulate the world with a wide range of skin tones. His sons (Shem, Ham, and Japheth) could have been of different

---

[111] 2 Peter 2:4 (KJV): "For if God spared not the angels that sinned, but cast them down to hell, and delivered them into chains of darkness, to be reserved unto judgment."

[112] Jude 1:14–15 (KJV). Jude directly quotes from 1 Enoch 1:9, identifying Enoch as "the seventh from Adam" and calling him a prophet. This is one of the clearest New Testament validations of the Book of Enoch as a recognized prophetic source in the early church.

complexions, explaining the diversity of humanity without requiring any later additions to the human gene pool. On the other hand, if Noah were a European or Caucasian albino, his children would all have white skin—a conclusion at odds with the genetic diversity we observe in early post-flood civilizations across Africa, Asia, and the so-called Middle East.

The spread of human diversity is also connected to early post-flood migration. Genesis 10:25 mentions the days of Peleg, when "the earth was divided."[113] Some interpret this as a major landmass division. If early humans once lived closer together before this separation, the descendants of Noah would have spread across different regions, carrying their genetic traits, languages, and cultures with them. This framework helps explain how a single ancestral line could have given rise to the wide range of human appearances seen today.

Who Are the Gentiles?

> *"Now these are the generations of the sons of Noah, Shem, Ham, and Japheth: and unto them were sons born after the flood. The sons of Japheth; Gomer, and Magog, and Madai, and Javan, and Tubal, and Meshech, and Tiras—By these were the isles of the Gentiles divided in their lands; every one after his tongue, after their families, in their nations" (Genesis 10:1–5, KJV).*[114]

---

[113] Genesis 10:25 (KJV): "And unto Eber were born two sons: the name of one was Peleg; for in his days was the earth divided." The Hebrew word peleg means "division." Some interpret this as referring to the division of languages at Babel; others suggest a physical division of landmasses.

[114] Genesis 10:1–5 (KJV). The Table of Nations in Genesis 10 is widely recognized as one of the oldest ethnographic documents. See D. J. Wiseman, "Genesis 10: Some

Dr. Linda Searight, in her book *Your Pastor Has Failed You: The Truth About Israel*, argues that Europeans rewrote Jewish history and falsely claimed descent from the ancient Israelites.[115] She states that Zionist Jews, including the Rothschild dynasty, now control Israel, where conflict continues between Arabs and European Jews. She notes, however, that the land of Canaan was not promised to Ishmael's descendants, though God did bless Ishmael to become a great nation.

Dr. Eran Elhaik, a geneticist at the Johns Hopkins School of Public Health, explored the historical origins of European Jewry in his Oxford-published study titled *"The Missing Link of Jewish European Ancestry: Contrasting the Rhineland and the Khazarian Hypotheses."*[116] In this research, Elhaik critically examined genetic and forensic evidence and concluded that his findings support the Khazarian Hypothesis, which asserts that many modern Ashkenazi Jews are descendants of the Khazars—a Turkic people who lived in a powerful medieval empire between the Black and Caspian Seas and who converted to Judaism during the early medieval period. It is important to note that other prominent geneticists have contested Elhaik's conclusions, and the Khazarian hypothesis remains a subject of active scholarly debate; however, that is to be expected.

Archaeological Considerations," Journal of the Transactions of the Victoria Institute 87 (1955): 14–24.

[115] Linda Searight, Your Pastor Has Failed You: The Truth About Israel (self-published). Searight's work argues that modern European Jews are not descended from the ancient Israelites and that their claim to the land of Israel is based on political Zionism rather than biblical lineage.

[116] Eran Elhaik, "The Missing Link of Jewish European Ancestry: Contrasting the Rhineland and the Khazarian Hypotheses," Genome Biology and Evolution 5, no. 1 (January 2013): 61–74, doi:10.1093/gbe/evs119. Published by Oxford University Press.

After the fall of Jerusalem in 70 AD and the banishment, the Hebrews fled to Africa to escape Roman persecution. At the same time, Edomite converts moved north to regions resembling their appearance, likely Khazaria (modern-day Ukraine). Ashkenazi Jews trace their lineage to Japheth rather than Israel, while Edomites descend from Esau—Semitic but distinct from Jacob-Israel's descendants. By the 16th century, "Jew" came to refer to both converts and bloodline Israelites, blending identities. Today, most Jews in Palestine are of Ashkenazi and European descent, whereas the true Judeans are black North East Africans, tied to the birthright through Jacob's twelve sons.

The history of the Khazars is not a myth, nor is it a baseless conspiracy theory—it is a documented part of world history. Historical accounts, archaeological findings, and references in multiple medieval sources confirm their existence and influence. In Arthur Koestler's book *The Thirteenth Tribe (1976)*, he presents the controversial theory that modern Ashkenazi Jews are descendants of the Khazars.[117] He portrays the Khazars as a wealthy and influential kingdom that functioned as a buffer between the Byzantine Empire and the Muslim Caliphates. By controlling key trade routes between Europe and Asia, the empire became a major hub for commerce and diplomacy. Its population was highly diverse, comprising Turkic tribes, Slavs, and other groups.

---

[117] Arthur Koestler, The Thirteenth Tribe: The Khazar Empire and Its Heritage (London: Hutchinson, 1976). Koestler's thesis is that Ashkenazi Jews descend primarily from the Khazars, a semi-nomadic Turkic people whose ruling class is believed to have converted to Judaism in the early medieval period.

Seeking the true faith, King Bulan, the Khazar ruler, invited representatives of Christianity, Islam, and Judaism to debate before him. According to Arthur Koestler's account, he ultimately chose to convert to Judaism in the eighth or ninth century, viewing it as a neutral position between his Christian and Muslim neighbors.[118] Following his conversion, he invited Jewish rabbis from Babylon and other regions to teach the Khazars the laws, customs, and beliefs of Judaism. They instructed the people in the Torah and the Talmud, established synagogues, and introduced the language and traditions of the faith. However, this form of Judaism was influenced by Babylonian mystery religions rather than the original Torah. Over time, Jewish sects such as the Karaites, Kabbalists, and Hasidim developed, creating a distinct religious identity distinct from true Israelite worship.

By the late sixth century CE, the Khazars had established a powerful commercial empire spanning parts of southeastern European Russia and the Caucasus region. Historical and archaeological evidence suggests they were originally connected to the western branch of the Turkic Empire, which extended into Turkistan. However, aspects of their early history and the origin of their name remain debated. Because of this background, some historians and genetic researchers have proposed that portions of the Ashkenazi Jewish population may descend in part from Gentile converts such as the Khazars rather than exclusively from ancient Semitic lineages. Supporters of this theory cite linguistic, cultural, and historical references, including Assyrian

[118] Arthur Koestler, *The Thirteenth Tribe: The Khazar Empire and Its Heritage* (New York: Random House, 1976), 38–45.

inscriptions that mention a people called the Ashkuza, who clashed with the Assyrian Empire during Esarhaddon's reign.

Centuries later, Ashkenazi Jews became highly influential in the rise of modern Zionism during the late nineteenth century. This movement sought to establish a Jewish homeland in historic Palestine and ultimately contributed to the founding of the State of Israel in 1948. The 1905 edition of the Jewish Encyclopedia also noted that the overwhelming majority of the world's Jewish population at that time was Ashkenazi.[119]

Image 11 – Jews paying homage at the Western Wall.

Identifying the nations requires examining people groups and tracing their origins back to the progenitors, specifically the three

[119] The Jewish Encyclopedia (1901–1906), s.v. "Statistics," noted the predominance of Ashkenazi Jews among world Jewry. By the early 20th century, Ashkenazi Jews constituted roughly 90% of the global Jewish population.

sons of Noah. According to the Table of Nations and Genealogy of Mankind and my research on people groups, these are the approximate breakdowns of Noah's three sons.[120] While this may not be 100% accurate, I believe it is predominantly accurate. However, further research only enhances our knowledge and understanding of who's who.

Japheth's name means "opened," "enlarged," "fair," or "light." He is traditionally regarded as the ancestor of the Indo-European or Caucasoid peoples, whose descendants spread widely across Europe and parts of Asia. His sons became the forefathers of many nations: Gomer is linked to Celtic, Germanic, and Western European peoples; Magog to groups in Russia and Eastern Europe; Madai to the Medes, Persians, and related Iranian and Central Asian peoples; and Javan to the Greeks and many Mediterranean and southern European nations. Tubal, Meshech, and Tiras are associated with peoples of the Caucasus, Eastern Europe, and Scandinavia. Together, Japheth's lineage is commonly connected with the formation of many European and Indo-European cultures.

> *"God shall enlarge Japheth, and he shall dwell in the tents of Shem; and Canaan shall be his servant" (Genesis 9:27, KJV).*

Is Japheth Dwelling in the Tents of Shem?

An article published by Al Jazeera on May 15, 2017, under the title *"The Nakba Did Not Start or End in 1948,"* stated that when Israel

[120] Table of Nations and Genealogy of Mankind. An online genealogical compilation that presents traditional interpretations of the descendants of Noah's sons (Shem, Ham, and Japheth) and attempts to correlate them with various historical and ethnic groups. See "Table of Nations and Genealogy of Mankind," in *The Oldest Books in the World*, RootsWeb Freepages, accessed May 8, 2026.

became a state in 1948, many Palestinians were violently forced from their homeland. This movement was led by Zionists, resulting in Palestinians becoming refugees and the land undergoing ethnic displacement.[121]

The word "enlarge" in Noah's prophecy concerning his son Japheth is translated from the Hebrew word *pathah* (paw-thaw), as found in Strong's Exhaustive Concordance.[122] This word carries a wide range of meanings, including alluring, deceiving, enlarging, enticing, flattering, and persuading. While "enlarge" might sound like a blessing, the deeper Hebrew meaning suggests a more complex picture—possibly even a warning. In various parts of Scripture, pathah is associated with seduction or deception. With that in mind, Noah's prophecy could suggest that Japheth would be influenced (perhaps even deceived) into dwelling in a place that was not originally his. That place, according to the prophecy, is the "tents of Shem." The phrase "dwelling in the tents of Shem" has often been misinterpreted, but I believe it literally refers to inhabiting the land or inheritance of Shem's descendants.

This shift occurred through two major developments:

1. **The intermingling of Japheth's and Esau's lineages:** Over time, the descendants of Japheth (often associated with European nations) and Esau (Edomites) merged through

---

[121] Al Jazeera, "The Nakba Did Not Start or End in 1948," May 15, 2017. The term Nakba ("catastrophe" in Arabic) refers to the displacement of approximately 700,000 Palestinians during the 1948 Arab-Israeli War and the establishment of the State of Israel.

[122] Strong's Exhaustive Concordance, H6601: pathah (paw-thaw'), meaning "to open, to be spacious, to be wide." In various scriptural contexts, the word carries connotations of enticement, persuasion, or deception. See Exodus 22:16 (seduction); Deuteronomy 11:16 (deception); Judges 14:15 (enticement).

intermarriage and cultural assimilation. This blending gave rise to a people who would eventually claim identity and inheritance that, biblically, did not belong to them.

2. **The re-establishment of the state of Israel in 1948:** Following World War II, many Ashkenazi Jews (who trace their lineage through Europe and are predominantly of Japhetic origin) were relocated to the land historically promised to Shem's descendants, particularly the Israelites. This geopolitical event solidified the physical and political occupation of a land originally covenanted to Shem's seed.

So today, we witness a fulfillment of Noah's ancient prophecy: a people, largely of Japhetic descent, dwelling in the land meant for Shem's lineage. If the descendants of Japheth are identified as the Gentiles, and the Gentiles later became the European nations, then this would imply that Europeans who claim to be Jews are not actually Israelites by lineage, but are instead Gentiles according to biblical classification. This raises deeper questions about identity, prophecy, and inheritance. Who truly are the descendants of Shem? And what does this mean for the future as biblical prophecy continues to unfold? Before we answer these questions, let us take a look at Ham and his descendants.

> *"And the sons of Ham; Cush, and Mizraim, and Phut, and Canaan—And Cush begat Nimrod: he began to be a mighty one in the earth" (Genesis 10:6; 8, KJV).*

Ham, whose name means "hot," "burnt," or "dark," is traditionally viewed as the ancestor of many African and other non-European peoples. His descendants, known as the Hamites, spread widely across Africa and neighboring regions. His sons became the forefathers of numerous nations: Canaan is linked to the ancient peoples of the Levant; Cush to groups in regions like Ethiopia and Nubia; Mizraim to the Egyptians and Copts; and Phut to North African peoples such as the Libyans and Berbers. Through these lines, Ham's descendants spread across Africa, parts of the so-called Middle East, and surrounding regions.

Babel, Erech, and Akkad all lie in southern Iraq—the heartland of the ancient Mesopotamian civilization. These three cities were part of what was known in cuneiform texts as "the Land of Sumer and Akkad."[123] Together, they formed the world's first empire, established by Nimrod. Sumer is where we get the term "Sumerians"—the first known civilization in the region, flourishing from around 4100–1750 BC.

Nimrod, also known as Nimroud-bar-Cush in ancient monuments, was the grandson of Ham. The meaning of Ham's name (hot, burnt, or dark) is significant, as it connects him to the lineage traditionally associated with the Mongoloid and African peoples. The Egyptian name Khem, from which the word Kemet is derived, also reflects this imagery, translating to "swarthy," "darkened," or, more literally, "the sun-burnt."[124] These descriptions align with the idea that Ham's descendants settled in regions with darker complexions and hotter

---

123 The Sumerian civilization flourished in southern Mesopotamia (modern-day Iraq) from approximately 4100–1750 BC. Cities such as Ur, Uruk, and Eridu are among the oldest known urban centers. See Samuel Noah Kramer, The Sumerians: Their History, Culture, and Character (Chicago: University of Chicago Press, 1963).

124 Kemet (Egyptian: kmt) is the ancient Egyptian name for Egypt, meaning "black land," referring to the dark, fertile soil of the Nile floodplain. The term has also been interpreted as a reference to the people themselves. See Erik Hornung, History of Ancient Egypt: An Introduction (Ithaca, NY: Cornell University Press, 1999).

climates. Ham fathered Cush, whose name means "blackness," and Cush fathered Nimrod.

Let me elaborate on Flavius Josephus, whom I have mentioned in earlier chapters.[125] Born Joseph ben Matthias in Jerusalem around 37 AD and passing away in Rome around AD 100, he was a Hebrew priest, scholar, and historian descended from the Maccabees. He is best known for his significant writings on the Jewish revolt of 66–70 AD and for his accounts of earlier Hebrew history. Highly esteemed by the Romans, Josephus was commissioned by the emperor to record and preserve the history of the Hebrew people.

According to Josephus in *Antiquities of the Jews*, Chapter 4, the three sons of Noah were born a hundred years before the flood.[126] After the flood, they were the first to descend from the mountains into the plains and settle there. The area where they initially settled was called Shinar. God commanded them to send out colonies to populate the earth so that they would not overcrowd or create conflict among themselves. However, due to their poor understanding, they disobeyed God's commands. As their population grew and they prospered, they continued to rebel against the Most-High's commands. At the center of this defiance was Nimrod, the grandson of Ham. A strong and courageous man, Nimrod inspired the people to reject the idea that their blessings came from God. He persuaded

[125] Flavius Josephus (born Joseph ben Matthias, c. 37–100 AD) was a first-century Jewish priest, scholar, and historian. His major works include *Wars of the Jews* and *Antiquities of the Jews*, the latter being a comprehensive history of the Jewish people from creation to the first century. The Roman Emperor Vespasian commissioned him to record Jewish history. See Tessa Rajak, Josephus: The Historian and His Society (London: Duckworth, 1983).
[126] Josephus, *Antiquities of the Jews*, 1.4. Josephus records the post-flood settlement of Noah's sons and Nimrod's rise to power. See William Whiston, trans—The Works of Josephus (Peabody, MA: Hendrickson, 1987).

them to believe that their own strength and bravery were the sources of their success. Over time, Nimrod converted the government into a tyranny, declaring that if God ever tried to flood the world again, he would build a tower so tall that the floodwaters would never reach the people.

In the Book of Jasher, Chapter 9, we get more clarity about what happened at the Tower of Babel.[127] During King Nimrod's reign, the entire earth was united in language and purpose. Nimrod and his princes (Phut, Mizraim, Cush, and Canaan) planned to build a grand city with a towering structure that would reach heaven. Their goal was to make a name for themselves, prevent being scattered, and dominate all nations. Around 600,000 people gathered in the valley of Shinar, where they settled and began making bricks. As construction progressed, the people divided into three groups: one sought to fight God in heaven, another wanted to place their own gods there, and the third aimed to attack heaven with weapons. God intervened by commanding seventy angels to confuse the people's language, causing chaos and violence among the builders. God punished the three rebellious factions according to their intentions. The site was named Babel, meaning "confusion," as it marked the division of languages across the world. From this place, all of the great ancient empires arose.

---

[127] The Book of Jasher (Sefer HaYashar), Chapter 9. The Book of Jasher is referenced in Joshua 10:13 and 2 Samuel 1:18 as a source known to biblical authors. The surviving text, printed in Hebrew in 1613, contains accounts that supplement biblical narratives. See J. H. Parry & Company, trans. The Book of Jasher (Salt Lake City, 1887).

"And Canaan begat Sidon his firstborn, and Heth, and the Jebusite, and the Amorite, and the Girgasite, and the Hivite, and the Arkite, and the Sinite, and the Arvadite, and the Zemarite, and the Hamathite: and afterward were the families of the Canaanites spread abroad." (Genesis 10:15–18, KJV).

Some historical and biblical traditions connect two of Canaan's sons (Heth and Sin) with the origins of certain ancient peoples. Heth is commonly identified as the ancestor of the Hittites, also known as the Hatti or Chatti. Sin, listed in biblical genealogies as Heth's brother and linked to the Sinites, has been associated in some traditions with populations in the Far East. Classical writers used names like Sinae or Sinim to describe distant regions in the Far East. The Greek geographer Claudius Ptolemy used these terms to refer to territories believed to be in or around ancient China. Likewise, Isaiah 49:12 mentions the Sinim as a far-off people, which some interpreters take to refer to populations in the distant East.[128] Although modern historians and linguists generally question the idea that Sin was a literal ancestor of East Asian peoples, the repeated appearance of the "Sin" root in ancient names for China shows how early cultures used language, tradition, and distant knowledge to describe one of the world's oldest civilizations.

As stated in the Zondervan Compact Bible Dictionary, Ham is the youngest son of Noah, born about 96 years before the flood, and one of eight persons to survive the flood. He became "the progenitor of

[128] Isaiah 49:12 (KJV): "Behold, these shall come from far: and, lo, these from the north and from the west; and these from the land of Sinim."

the dark races; NOT THE NEGROES, but the Egyptians, Ethiopians, Libyans, and Canaanites."[129]

In 1787, Constantin-François de Chassebœuf, comte de Volney, published reflections from a journey through Ottoman-ruled Egypt.[130] During his travels, he recorded observations about the physical features of the Egyptian people, noting their facial characteristics and comparing them to what he described as "mulatto" traits. While studying ancient monuments, Volney believed he found further support for his conclusions upon examining the Great Sphinx of Giza. He argued that the Sphinx's facial features resembled what he identified as African characteristics. Reflecting on Herodotus's writings, which described certain ancient populations as dark-skinned with woolly hair, Volney concluded that the ancient Egyptians were closely related to other African peoples. His reflections reveal how his encounter with Egypt's people and monuments challenged prevailing European assumptions about the racial identity of ancient civilizations, suggesting a deeply African origin for the builders of Egypt's ancient glory. Egypt may be predominantly Arab in terms of nationality because of Arab conquests; however, geographically, it is African.

---

[129] Zondervan Compact Bible Dictionary, ed. T. Alton Bryant (Grand Rapids: Zondervan, 1967), s.v. "Ham." The entry identifies Ham as "the progenitor of the dark races; not the Negroes, but the Egyptians, Ethiopians, Libyans, and Canaanites."

[130] Constantin-François de Chassebœuf, comte de Volney, Voyage en Égypte et en Syrie (Paris, 1787). English translation: Travels Through Syria and Egypt in the Years 1783, 1784, and 1785, 2 vols. (London: G. G. J. and J. Robinson, 1787). Volney's observations on the Sphinx's physical features and the Egyptian people were influential in early discussions of the ancient Egyptians' racial identity.

Why Were Black People Identified with Canaan?

To answer that question, we must look at Genesis 9:18–29. After the flood, Noah became a farmer and planted a vineyard. One day, he drank too much wine, became drunk, and lay uncovered in his tent. Ham, one of Noah's sons, "saw his father's nakedness" and told his two brothers, Shem and Japheth. The brothers took a garment, laid it over both their shoulders, walked backward, and covered their father's nakedness. When Noah awoke and learned what had happened, he cursed Ham's son Canaan, declaring that he would be a servant to his brothers, and he blessed Shem and Japheth.

At first glance, this raises an obvious question: if Ham committed the offense, why was Canaan cursed rather than Ham?

Several explanations have been offered throughout history. Some suggest that Noah, speaking prophetically, foresaw the future wickedness of Canaan and his descendants. Others argue that the judgment reflects a principle of measure-for-measure justice: because Noah was dishonored by one of his sons, Ham would experience dishonor through one of his own sons. Another explanation points to Genesis 9:1, where God had already blessed Noah and all his sons (including Ham) after the Flood. Since Ham had already received God's blessing, some believe the curse could not fall directly on him and therefore fell on Canaan instead.

While each of these theories has merit, the explanation that accounts for the most biblical details is that Ham committed a sexual sin involving Noah's wife and that Canaan was conceived as a result of that incestuous relationship.

To understand the context of this incident, we must examine the Scriptures. Leviticus 18:7–8 warns against uncovering the nakedness of one’s father or mother, equating it with dishonoring one’s father. Leviticus 20:11 affirms that if a man lies with his father’s wife, he has uncovered his father’s nakedness—an offense that merits death. Leviticus 20:17 addresses incest between siblings. Deuteronomy 27:20 echoes this, stating that a man shall not take his father’s wife, so that he does not uncover his father’s nakedness. These passages reveal that “uncovering nakedness” is often a biblical expression for sexual relations, particularly incest.

Based on this understanding, many interpret Ham’s act not merely as seeing Noah unclothed but as committing a sexual offense possibly involving Noah’s wife. If so, Canaan may have been the result of that act, making him both Ham’s son and a maternal half-brother to Shem and Japheth. If this interpretation is correct, it also explains why Canaan (not Ham) became the object of Noah's curse. Canaan would have been the living evidence of Ham's sin, born from an incestuous union. This understanding answers the question that the other theories leave unresolved.

It also sheds light on Noah's statement that Canaan would serve "his brethren." Genesis 9:25 declares, "Cursed be Canaan; a servant of servants shall he be unto his brethren." The very next verses identify those brethren as Shem and Japheth (Genesis 9:26–27). While Canaan was certainly Ham's son, this language also makes sense if he was born to Noah's wife, making him not only Ham's son but also the maternal half-brother of Shem and Japheth. Although Scripture never explicitly states this, it offers a coherent explanation for why the text repeatedly emphasizes his relationship to them in this way.

Regardless of which interpretation one ultimately accepts, one truth is beyond dispute: the curse was pronounced only upon Canaan and his descendants—not upon Ham's entire lineage. The phrase "servant of servants" denotes the lowest form of servitude imaginable, yet Noah never pronounced this judgment over Cush, Mizraim, or Put. Canaan's descendants settled in the region that bore his name—the Land of Canaan. This was the very territory God later promised to Abraham, a descendant of Shem. Centuries later, Joshua conquered the land and forced the Canaanites into labor. In Solomon's day, the surviving Canaanites were still subjected to a similar form of servitude. In this way, the prophetic word over Canaan was fulfilled with precision.

> *"And he said, Cursed be Canaan; a servant of servants shall he be unto his brethren. And he said, Blessed be the Lord God of Shem; and Canaan shall be his servant. God shall enlarge Japheth, and he shall dwell in the tents of Shem; and Canaan shall be his servant" (Genesis 9:25–27, KJV).*

Sadly, this passage has been grossly misapplied throughout history. The false teaching that all of Ham's descendants (especially Africans) were cursed has no biblical foundation. Scripture makes it abundantly clear that the curse was limited to Canaan and his lineage, not to the peoples of Cush, Mizraim, or Put. This long-standing misconception has fueled unjust racial prejudices and must be firmly rejected in light of the truth revealed in God's Word.

This curse was used to confuse and to explain why the so-called African American has endured so much oppression, and to provide a reason for our dark skin as if it were a curse—but these are nothing but lies. How can our dark skin be a curse when it is the result of melanin, which also indicates dominant genetics?[131]

Remember: when God made mankind from the dust of the ground, He said, "This is very good!" His creation was not the result of a malfunction, but was complete, with all the necessary components for life. Do not allow the enemy to keep perpetuating lies that make you feel inferior. You are made in the image and likeness of the Most-High.

> *"Unto Shem also, the father of all the children of Eber, the brother of Japheth the elder, even to him were children born. The children of Shem: Elam, and Asshur, and Arphaxad, and Lud, and Aram" (Genesis 10:21–22, KJV).*

Shem, whose name means "name" or "renown," is the source of the terms *Semitic* and *Shemitic*. He is regarded as the ancestor of many ancient Near Eastern peoples. His sons founded several nations:

Elam became the forefather of the Elamites and part of the Persian line; Asshur, of the Assyrians; Arphaxad, of the Chaldeans, Babylonians, Hebrews, and many Arab peoples; Lud, of groups in Asia Minor; and Aram, of the Arameans and Syrians.

Shem is also traditionally seen as the ancestor of Eber, from whom the term "Hebrew" is believed to derive. Abraham, a descendant of Eber, is the first person in Scripture called a Hebrew. From Abraham came Isaac and Ishmael—Isaac becoming the ancestor of the

---

[131] In general, genetic variants associated with higher melanin production tend to be dominant over many variants associated with lighter skin. Consequently, dark skin is a normal expression of human genetic inheritance and adaptation, not a mark of divine judgment or a consequence of the curse pronounced upon Canaan.

Israelites and Ishmael the forefather of many Arab peoples. Both lines are considered Semitic and share common linguistic and ancestral roots. In general usage, "*Semitic*" refers to people who speak Semitic languages such as Hebrew, Arabic, Aramaic, or Akkadian. "*Shemitic*," however, more specifically refers to those genealogically descended from Shem in Genesis. This distinction shows the difference between a linguistic category and a genealogical one.

This is why understanding the historical and linguistic context is so important. The world has been manipulated, with people believing that any negative mention of Jews or Judaism equates to antisemitism. However, if we consider the literal meaning of "anti-Semitic," it would refer to being against the Semitic languages or peoples descended from Shem. For example, Ashkenazi Jews primarily speak Yiddish—a language that originated as a German dialect and later incorporated elements from Hebrew and several other modern languages. Because Hebrew was the original language of the ancient Israelites, Yiddish does not qualify as a Semitic language. Furthermore, from a genealogical perspective, Ashkenazi Jews are often traced to populations associated with Japheth rather than Shem.

The name "Ashkenaz," from which they derive their identity, refers to a descendant of Japheth and is traditionally linked in Hebrew sources to the land of Germany.[132] Ultimately, it is through the Shemitic line

---

[132] The name *Ashkenaz* first appears in Bible, Genesis 10:3 and 1 Chronicles 1:6 as a grandson of Japheth through Gomer. In later rabbinic tradition, particularly Genesis Rabbah 37:1, "Ashkenaz" became identified with Germania (Germany), from which the term "Ashkenazi" came to designate Jews living in Germany and, later, Central and Eastern Europe. See also Encyclopaedia Judaica, s.v. "Ashkenaz."

(specifically through Abraham, Isaac, and Jacob) that the tribes of Israel descend, and from this lineage, the Messiah was born.

> *"And he made from one man every nation of mankind to live on all the face of the earth, having determined allotted periods and the boundaries of their dwelling place" Acts 17:26 (ESV).*[133]

After the flood, Noah's sons became the progenitors of all people on earth. The Bible tells us that the families of the three patriarchs migrated to various regions, and history supports this movement. Moreover, archaeological and genetic evidence indicate that Indigenous peoples inhabited the Americas for thousands of years before Christopher Columbus arrived in 1492.[134] In fact, when Columbus arrived, he brought a Hebrew interpreter. Luis de Torres was a converso (Jewish convert to Christianity) who spoke Hebrew, Aramaic, Spanish, Portuguese, French, Latin, and some Arabic. Columbus specifically included de Torres because he spoke Hebrew—Columbus believed he would encounter Hebrew-speaking peoples on the other side of the world.[135] He expected to find the "ten lost tribes of Israel" there, so having a Hebrew speaker was essential to him.

---

133 In Acts 17:26, the apostle Paul the Apostle speaks to the philosophers of Athens at the Areopagus, explaining that all nations descended from one origin under God's sovereign authority. The verse emphasizes that God governs humanity by establishing nations, determining their historical periods, and setting the boundaries of their lands, thereby demonstrating His rule over all peoples rather than any single ethnic group.

134 Indigenous peoples lived throughout North and South America long before Christopher Columbus arrived in 1492, having migrated and established civilizations across the continents thousands of years earlier. See Ivan Van Sertima, *They Came Before Columbus* (New York: Random House, 1976).

135 See Cecil Roth, "The Jews and the Discovery of America," in A History of the Jews in England (Oxford: Clarendon Press, 1941). Luis de Torres, Columbus's interpreter, was a converso (Jewish convert to Christianity) who spoke Hebrew,

You must know who you are! You are not adopted. Despite challenges and confusion, we are not without identity. We are descendants of Shem (the true Shemites) and descendants of the Hebrews of the Bible. Yet various factors have caused many of us to experience an identity crisis and lose knowledge of who we truly are. Without proper understanding, it is easy to be misled or confused, but this book aims to correct that misunderstanding. As we explore the coming chapters, we will uncover how the Hebrews came to be cursed, oppressed, scattered across the world, and ultimately enslaved. May our true identity be awakened, reclaimed, and fully restored.

Aramaic, and Arabic. Columbus believed he might encounter Hebrew-speaking peoples and considered de Torres essential for communication.

CHAPTER FIVE

2 Nations

The story of Jacob and Esau is one of the most compelling narratives in the book of Genesis, rich with themes of family, rivalry, deception, and reconciliation. It begins with the birth of twin brothers to Isaac and Rebekah, descendants of Abraham, God's chosen patriarch. Even before their birth, a divine prophecy revealed that the older would serve the younger, setting the stage for a lifelong struggle between the two.

In Genesis 25:20–25, Isaac married Rebekah when he was forty years old. When she was unable to have children, Isaac prayed, and God answered by allowing her to conceive. During her pregnancy, the children struggled within her, prompting Rebekah to seek the Most-High. God revealed that two nations were in her womb and that two distinct peoples would come from her, with the older serving the younger. When the time came for her to give birth, she delivered twins, and the firstborn was red and very hairy, so he was named Esau.

Notice the emphasis on Esau's description but no mention of Jacob's description. This is because Jacob looked like everyone else. We must understand that whenever the skin or appearance differed, the Bible described and emphasized it. For example, in Numbers 12:10, Miriam became "leprous, white as snow" as divine punishment.[136] Also, in Exodus 4:6, God turned Moses's hand "leprous as snow" as a sign.[137] It is interesting that in these instances concerning Moses, white skin represented a curse or a significant change. The Scriptures above are clear indicators that white skin was considered leprous and also something totally out of the norm for this population. This is something that has changed in meaning over time: the leprosy we know today is a curable bacterial infection, whereas the leprosy described in the Bible referred to a condition marked by white skin, skin patches, peeling, or blistering.

In Genesis 25:29–34, Esau returned from the field exhausted and hungry and found Jacob cooking a red lentil stew. Desperate for food, Esau begged Jacob for some. Seizing the opportunity, Jacob offered the stew only if Esau agreed to sell him his birthright—the special privileges and inheritance due to the firstborn son. Driven by immediate hunger, Esau rashly agreed, saying, *"I am about to die—of what use is a birthright to me?"* He swore an oath and sold his birthright for a meal. Because of Esau's mindset toward his birthright, this became the very reason the Most-High allowed the transfer. Esau did not see it as important. He did not reverence it, and his fleshly desire was the driving force behind his actions.

The spirit of Esau still influences the world today, encouraging people to satisfy their desires in the moment without thinking about the

---

[136] Numbers 12:10 (KJV). Miriam was struck with leprosy, "white as snow," as divine punishment for speaking against Moses. The Hebrew word tsara'ath, translated "leprosy," described various skin conditions marked by whitening, scaling, or discoloration—distinct from Hansen's disease (modern leprosy). See Jacob Milgrom, Leviticus 1–16, Anchor Bible (New York: Doubleday, 1991).
[137] Exodus 4:6 (KJV). God gave Moses a sign by turning his hand "leprous as snow" when placed in his bosom, then restoring it to its original color.

future. This mindset promotes immediate gratification but often results in regret. Hebrews 12:16–17 warns against being like Esau, who sold his birthright for a single meal and later couldn't regain the blessing, even though he sought it with tears. In contrast, Jacob valued the birthright because he understood the blessing it conferred. The birthright also represented the lineage through which the Messiah would come, a line set apart for God's divine purpose.

The birthright carried deep spiritual significance and was directly tied to the Messianic promise. In the patriarchal culture, the birthright was not just about receiving a double portion of inheritance or family leadership; it represented the covenant blessing God gave to Abraham. That blessing included the Promised Land, nationhood (becoming a great people), and the spiritual promise that through Abraham's seed, all nations of the earth would be blessed.

Jacob (Esau's brother) was not perfect. He was a deceiver, a schemer, and at times, manipulative. But here is the difference: Jacob valued the blessing. He wanted what God had to offer. And God can work with that kind of desire. The seed of Jacob is marked by hunger for God—even if it comes through struggle. When Jacob wrestled with the angel in Genesis Chapter 32, he declared, *"I will not let you go until you bless me."* That tenacity is what God honors. God did not choose Jacob because he was perfect; He chose him because Jacob pursued what Esau carelessly threw away. We should be asking ourselves: are we pursuing God's righteousness, or do we care more about our own desires?

In the Bible, the patriarchal family structure emphasized the firstborn, especially the firstborn son. In the ancient Eastern world, the firstborn son was the representative of the family's authority or future authority. He would act as the authority whenever the father was not around. He was also given honor and a double portion of the inheritance. However, God oftentimes went against this order, and the blessing was transferred to the younger child, as seen with Joseph, Moses, David, Abraham, Jacob, Isaac, Solomon, and others.

Rebekah had twins, and the Hebrew historian Josephus records that, prophetically, two nations would take on the names of these boys. It was prophesied that the second-born was to exceed the first-born. The father loved Esau (whose name reflected his roughness), but his mother loved Jacob. Because Rebekah understood the importance of the birthright and the blessing, she sought to maneuver so that Jacob would obtain them. The father's blessing was a prophetic one, believed to have come from the Most-High. Therefore, once pronounced, it was established.

According to *The Legends of the Jews* by Louis Ginzberg, it was through Shem that the Most-High spoke to Rebekah, giving her guidance concerning her two sons.[138] Remarkably, Shem's words were deeply prophetic. He foretold that Vespasian would destroy the Temple—a prophecy fulfilled when Vespasian became Emperor during the destruction of Jerusalem. Shem also mentioned Solomon, who would not be born for many generations. Additionally, he referenced Rome, which at that time did not yet exist as a nation. He declared that one son would surpass the other in strength. Esau

[138] Louis Ginzberg, The Legends of the Jews, trans. Henrietta Szold, 7 vols. (Philadelphia: Jewish Publication Society, 1909–1938), vol. 1, "Jacob and Esau." Ginzberg records the Jewish tradition that Shem, acting as a prophetic figure, spoke to Rebekah regarding the destinies of her two sons.

would initially dominate the world, but ultimately, Jacob would prevail and rule. Shem concluded with the statement: *"The older of the two will serve the younger, provided the younger is pure of heart; otherwise, the younger will be enslaved by the older."*

Interesting Facts About Esau/Edom

Esau's name means "hairy," while Edom (the name given to his descendants) means "red." This description highlights not only his physical characteristics but also symbolizes aspects of his personality. Esau was described as a "man of the field"—a rugged outdoorsman and skilled hunter—traits that sharply contrasted with his twin brother Jacob's more domestic and reserved nature. His defining characteristics included his redness and unusual hairiness, which set him apart physically and symbolically.

According to *The Legends of the Jews* by Louis Ginzberg, Esau was not circumcised as a child because his father, Isaac, believed his reddish complexion might be linked to a blood condition. Isaac planned to wait until Esau was around thirteen years old. However, when the time came, Esau refused the procedure, choosing rebellion over obedience.[139] This distinction is made between Jacob and Esau: while Jacob submitted to God's covenant through circumcision, Esau rejected it. The refusal of circumcision was not simply a medical decision but a spiritual statement—it revealed Esau's heart posture toward God. Esau's defiance continued when he married two

---

[139] Ginzberg, Legends of the Jews, vol. 1. The tradition that Esau refused circumcision at age thirteen is found in Jewish Midrashic literature. See also Genesis Rabbah 63:10.

Canaanite women without his father's permission, thereby directly opposing his family's traditions.[140]

The term Edom means "red," just as the name Esau also signifies "red."[141] This association links Esau/Edom to the color red, which carries deep symbolic meaning in both Scripture and historical context. In Scripture, red often represents bloodshed (2 Kings 3:22; Isaiah 1:15) and sin (Isaiah 1:18). The red horse in Revelation 6:4 represents war and conflict—and Esau was prophesied to live by the sword (Genesis 27:40). The red dragon in Revelation 12:3 symbolizes the satanic, anti-Christian system. The beast of Revelation, tied to global corruption and false religion, is scarlet-colored, and the woman who rides it is dressed in red (Revelation 17:3–4).[142] The Rothschild family, prominent in global banking and of Jewish descent, bears a name meaning "red shield."[143] The red flag is a symbol of socialism and revolution—movements historically influenced by Jewish figures.[144] In the Jewish Kabbalah, red is associated with both bloodshed and justice. And the historian Arthur

---

[140] Genesis 36:2 (KJV).

[141] Genesis 25:30 (KJV).

[142] The color red in Scripture is frequently associated with themes of bloodshed, sin, and conflict, as seen in passages such as Second Book of Kings 3:22 and Book of Isaiah 1:15, 18. In apocalyptic imagery, the red horse of Revelation 6:4 symbolizes war and violence, while the prophecy concerning Esau in Genesis 27:40 ("by thy sword shalt thou live") is often interpreted as reflecting a life marked by conflict. Additionally, the red dragon in Revelation 12:3 represents satanic opposition, and the scarlet-colored beast and the woman arrayed in red in Revelation 17:3–4 symbolize corruption, false religion, and worldly power; together, these passages contribute to a broader biblical motif in which red conveys violence, sin, and spiritual opposition.

[143] The Rothschild family, a prominent banking dynasty of Jewish heritage, derives its name from the German "Rothschild, meaning "red shield," originating from the house sign used by the family in Frankfurt during the 16th century.

[144] The red flag has long been a symbol of socialism and revolutionary movements, gaining prominence during the French Revolution and later becoming associated with labor movements and socialist ideology in the 19th and 20th centuries.

Koestler noted that the Khazars (ancestors of many modern Jews) were historically referred to as the "Red Jews."

Interesting Facts About Jacob

Jacob's name carries several meanings, including "to follow," "to be behind," and also "to supplant," "circumvent," or "overreach." It is also associated with the word for "heel," referencing the moment he grasped Esau's heel at birth. Jacob would become the father of a nation that would live by the Word (the Torah). Interestingly, there is no detailed physical description of Jacob in the biblical text, likely because he resembled the typical appearance of Hebrews, Ethiopians, or Egyptians of his time. Whenever the Bible gave a distinct description of someone, it was because they were something out of the ordinary.

Now, contrary to common belief, Jacob did not steal the birthright—Esau willingly gave it up. What Jacob did take, however, was the blessing of the firstborn, which traditionally belonged to Esau. Yet even that act did not change God's plan. Jacob did not actually need to deceive Isaac to receive the blessing, because the prophetic birthright was already destined for him. So, Jacob, the younger, received the blessing of the firstborn from their father, Isaac, through his act of deception. With his mother's help, Jacob disguised himself to look and smell like Esau. Isaac, whose eyesight had grown dim, was deceived and unknowingly gave Jacob the blessing meant for the firstborn, which included prosperity, leadership, and covenantal favor.

Though the method was deceptive, this event fulfilled God's earlier prophecy that "the older will serve the younger."[145]

It also revealed Jacob's deep desire for God's promises—something Esau did not fully grasp. Ultimately, Jacob's blessing set the course for him to become the father of the twelve tribes of Israel and the chosen line through which God's covenant would continue.

After Jacob left, Esau came home, prepared a savory meal, and brought it to his father. Isaac asked who he was, and when Esau revealed himself, Isaac trembled, knowing he had given the blessing to another. The Bible says that Esau cried and begged Isaac for a prophecy, so Isaac pronounced one on Esau that sounded like both a blessing and a curse:

> *"Behold, thy dwelling shall be the fatness of the earth, and of the dew of heaven from above; and by thy sword shalt thou live, and shalt serve thy brother; and it shall come to pass when thou shalt have the dominion, that thou shalt break his yoke from off thy neck" (Genesis 27:39–40, KJV).*

The significance of this prophecy is that Isaac tells Esau that he will live, abide, or make his habitation in the same place that was given to Jacob. This was not about Esau himself, but about his seed. His seed will dwell in the blessing of Jacob.

> *"Therefore thus saith the Lord God; Surely in the fire of my jealousy have I spoken against the residue of the heathen, and against all Idumea, which have appointed my land into*

[145] Genesis 25:23 (KJV).

their possession with the joy of all their heart, with despiteful minds, to cast it out for a prey" (Ezekiel 36:5).

This declaration reveals God's righteous anger against those who seek to claim what is not theirs, who take by force what He has set apart, and who rejoice in the oppression and displacement of His people. It is a warning that no act of conquest, deceit, or oppression escapes His notice. The history of Edom, and by extension the nations that followed in its footsteps, serves as a prophetic illustration: God will judge them for what they have done to His people and their Promised Land.

Esau hated Jacob and sought to kill him. Because of the tension between these two brothers, Isaac and Rebekah made them promise not to hurt each other. But in Jubilees 37:23, we glimpse Esau's mindset toward his brother. He says, *"And when the raven becomes white as the raza, then know that I have loved you and shall make peace with you. You shall be rooted out, and your sons shall be rooted out, and there shall be no peace for you."*[146] So, after Isaac prophesied to Esau, Esau, in his anger, promised Jacob that he would never have peace. According to the Book of Jasher 47:30-33, Esau took his wives, children, servants, livestock, and everything of value and left. According to Genesis 36:6–12, Esau departed to the hill country of Seir, among the Horites, and did not return to Canaan.[147]

---

[146] *Jubilees* 37:23 records Jacob's instruction to his sons concerning the dangers of intermarriage with the surrounding nations, emphasizing the importance of preserving their covenant identity and remaining separate from pagan customs and practices. This passage reflects a recurring theme throughout *Jubilees* that stresses faithfulness to God's covenant and the distinctiveness of the descendants of Abraham.

[147] Book of Jasher 47:30–33 records a traditional account of Pharaoh's fear of the Hebrews' rapid population growth in Egypt, paralleling the biblical narrative of oppression found in Exodus 1:8–14.

From there, Esau became the father of the Edomites, a nation that would stand in continual opposition to Israel throughout biblical history. His choice to leave the covenant land marked a spiritual separation as well, showing that while Jacob inherited the promise, Esau settled for temporal possessions and a legacy outside of God's chosen line.

According to Genesis, Esau married among the Canaanites, the Ishmaelites, the Hivites, the Hittites, and specifically the Horites. Esau also settled near Mount Seir, a region said to be inhabited by mysterious beings—neither fully human nor fully beast. These beings, including the Zuzim, Rephaim, Emim, Horites, Nephilim, and Anakim, were believed to result from unions between fallen angels and humans.

Mount Seir has historically been used to refer to three distinct regions, each with its own geographical and cultural significance. The first and most prominent is the mountainous territory east of the Arabah Valley, between the Dead Sea and the Gulf of Aqaba, originally inhabited by the Horites—cave-dwelling descendants of Seir, a Hamitic people. They were the original inhabitants of Idumea, a name later applied to Edom, and traced their lineage back to Hor, a descendant of Hivi, the son of Canaan. Eventually, they were displaced by Esau and his descendants, resulting in a mixed Horite-Edomite lineage and the establishment of the land of Edom.[148] The

[148] The Horites were among the original inhabitants of the region later known as Edom (also called Idumea), and are described in the Book of Genesis 36 as descendants of Seir the Horite, with figures such as Hor appearing in their lineage. The Horites are associated with the broader Canaanite world, often linked to the descendants of Canaan. Over time, the descendants of Esau came to inhabit Mount Seir, displacing or intermingling with the Horites (Deuteronomy 2:12), thereby establishing Edom and a blended Horite-Edomite presence in the region.

second reference appears in the territory of Judah (Joshua 15:10), marking part of Judah's northern boundary. The third, more speculative connection links Mount Seir to the Caucasus Mountains in the north, spanning modern southern Russia, Georgia, Armenia, and Azerbaijan. Some historical and theological interpretations suggest a symbolic or genealogical link between Esau's descendants and the peoples of the Caucasus, including the Khazars. However, this is not explicitly stated in the Bible.

Mount Seir exemplifies this layered history, referring to multiple regions—from the Horite homeland in Edom, to Judah's boundaries, to possible symbolic links with the Caucasus—reflecting a story of migration, identity, and interpretation across time.

Image 12 – Mountain Jews of the Caucasus.

Image 13 – Mountain Jews resting after a day's work.

Throughout history, Edom has engaged in calculated, multifaceted efforts to obscure its true lineage and identity. One of their primary methods has been the deliberate manipulation of historical records. By rewriting and reinterpreting documented events, they have systematically altered the historical narrative to align with their own objectives and solidify their fabricated legacy. This process often involved the strategic renaming of people, cultures, and regions to distort the collective memory of the past.

In addition to rewriting history, Edom has been instrumental in reshaping geographical boundaries. Maps have been redrawn, territories renamed, and borders shifted; all to legitimize their presence and obscure the ancestral claims of indigenous populations. In many cases, the original inhabitants of these lands were displaced or erased from the record entirely, only to be replaced by groups who physically and culturally resembled Edom themselves.

This calculated replacement served a dual purpose: not only did it facilitate their dominion over newly claimed lands, but it also enabled them to assume the identity and heritage of the people they supplanted. Over time, this deceitful practice led to the near-complete erasure of the authentic history and identity of numerous regions and civilizations, replacing them with a false narrative that continues to shape modern perceptions. In short, Edom's tactics have been comprehensive and deeply impactful, blending historical revisionism, territorial manipulation, and cultural appropriation to obscure their true origins and dominate the historical record. The Edomites often intermingled with other nations, likely attempting to conceal themselves, but God promised to expose them. Through Jeremiah, He declared that Edom could not hide from His judgment: their wisdom and counsel would fail, their attempts to flee or protect themselves would be in vain, and their secrets would be revealed. God's prophecy confirms that Esau's descendants would face calamity, and their lineage, neighbors, and allies would not escape His judgment (Jeremiah 49:7-10).

While Esau was away, dwelling in the mountains, Jacob married Rachel and Leah and had twelve sons. These twelve sons were named Reuben, Simeon, Levi, Judah, Dan, Naphtali, Gad, Asher, Issachar, Zebulun, Joseph, and Benjamin. From these twelve, we get the Children of Israel. In Exodus Chapter 1, the Children of Israel were living in Egypt. The journey of the Israelites into Egypt began when Joseph's brothers, out of jealousy, sold him to Ishmaelite traders. These traders then sold Joseph to Potiphar, an officer of Pharaoh in Egypt. After a series of trials (including being falsely accused and thrown into prison), Joseph's life took a dramatic turn when Pharaoh had a troubling dream. Joseph accurately interpreted the dream, leading to his promotion to second-in-command over all of Egypt. During a severe famine, Joseph brought his family to Egypt to preserve their lives, fulfilling God's greater plan. God used this entire situation not only to save His people but also to test them and reveal His power to the world's leading civilization at the time.

Years later, Joseph's brothers came to Egypt to buy grain to survive a famine. After revealing his identity to his brothers in Egypt, Joseph invites his father Jacob (Israel) and the entire family to move from Canaan to Egypt during the severe famine. Pharaoh, grateful for Joseph's service, welcomes the family and offers them the best land in Goshen. Jacob and around 70 family members make the journey, and Joseph is emotionally reunited with his father after many years. The family settles in Goshen, where they prosper under Joseph's protection, and Jacob meets Pharaoh and blesses him.

According to the Book of Jasher, when Jacob died, his sons went to bury their father in the cave of the Patriarchs, and Esau and his sons attempted to block Jacob's family, leading to a war in which Esau was killed. During the conflict, Esau's grandson Zepho was captured and taken to Egypt as a prisoner under Joseph. Still, Zepho later escaped and continued to harbor deep hatred toward the sons of Jacob.[149]

---

[149] Book of Jasher, Chapters 61–64. According to Jasher, Zepho (grandson of Esau through Eliphaz) fled to Chittim (associated with the Italian peninsula/Rome), where he was made king with the title Janus Saturnus. See also the entry on "Zepho" in the Josippon (10th-century Hebrew chronicle). The identification of Chittim with Rome is supported by Daniel 11:30 in the Septuagint.

Zepho fled to Africa, where he was welcomed as a formidable warrior and appointed captain of the army under King Angeas.[150] He persistently urged Angeas to wage war against Egypt and the Israelites. However, Angeas hesitated after witnessing the Israelites' strength firsthand. Among Angeas's servants was a young and wise sorcerer named Balaam, son of Beor, only fifteen years old.[151] Angeas asked Balaam to use witchcraft to predict the outcome of the battle, and the ritual revealed that Angeas's army would fall to the Israelites. Discouraged, Angeas abandoned his war plans. Seeing this, Zepho fled to Chittim (the original name for Rome), where he was welcomed and hired to lead their battles.

Zepho led a successful defense against African troops who were plundering Chittim for its resources. Impressed by his bravery, the people of Chittim made Zepho their king. As king, Zepho led them in wars against Tubal (the seed of Japheth) and nearby islands, conquering them. Zepho ruled over Chittim and the land of Italia for fifty years. King Zepho, son of Eliphaz, was called Janus Saturnus by his subjects.[152] Janus was a uniquely Roman deity, revered as the god of beginnings, transitions, endings, and duality. Unlike most Roman

---

[150] King Angeas (also rendered Agnias) appears in the Book of Jasher as a ruler of Africa (Carthage/Libya), a descendant of Phut, son of Ham, and father of Hannibal the Great. The connection to Hannibal Barca (247–183 BC), the famed Carthaginian general, appears in some medieval Jewish and extra-biblical traditions. Hannibal is historically remembered for crossing the Alps with war elephants during the Second Punic War (218–201 BC). See Adrian Goldsworthy, The Fall of Carthage: The Punic Wars 265–146 BC (London: Cassell, 2003).

[151] Book of Jasher, Chapters 61–64. Jasher identifies Balaam, son of Beor, as a young sorcerer in the service of King Angeas of Africa.

[152] Janus was a uniquely Roman deity with no Greek counterpart, revered as the god of beginnings, transitions, gates, and duality. He is typically depicted with two faces looking in opposite directions. The month of January (Latin: Ianuarius) is named after him. See Robert Turcan, The Gods of Ancient Rome: Religion in Everyday Life from Archaic to Imperial Times (New York: Routledge, 2001).

gods, Janus had no direct Greek counterpart. He was symbolically important for overseeing doorways, gates, and all forms of passages, both physical and symbolic. He is most famously depicted with two faces—one looking forward and the other backward—emphasizing his role as a guardian of transitions. The month of January (Ianuarius) is named after him.

Chittim, or Kittim, is the original name for the area of the Romans, but later expanded to include Greece and Macedonia.[153] According to the Book of Jasher, five years after the Israelites crossed the Jordan, a fierce conflict erupted between the children of Chittim and Edom. The Chittim army prevailed, ultimately subjugating Edom. From that point forward, the children of Chittim ruled Edom, and the two became one kingdom.[154] So, Esau's seed not only mixed with the Canaanites but also with the Horites, the nations of the seed of Japheth, and many others.

Regarding the conflict involving Egypt and Zepho, Egypt initially fought Zepho alone, fearing Israel might betray them. But after suffering heavy losses (about 210 soldiers), they called on Israel for help. Israel joined the battle with only 150 warriors against a vast alliance, while Egypt brought 3,000. Despite being outnumbered, Israel killed 2,000 enemies without losing a single man, causing fear to spread among Zepho's forces. However, the Egyptians fled mid-battle, leaving Israel to fight alone. Angered by this betrayal, Israel

---

[153] Jasher 10:16: "And the children of Chittim are the Romim who dwell in the valley of Canopia by the river Tibreu." This river is indeed the Tiber river that flows through Rome present day.

[154] Jasher 90:8-9: "And the children of Chittim ruled over Edom, and Edom became under the hand of the children of Chittim and became one kingdom from that day. And from that time they could no more lift up their heads, and their kingdom became one with the children of Chittim."

later killed some Egyptian soldiers they encountered and falsely blamed it on other nations. When Egypt discovered the truth, it became fearful of Israel's power.

After witnessing Israel's increasing strength and recent victories in battle, Pharaoh's counselors and Egypt's elders gathered before the king to express concern. They warned that the Israelites had become more powerful and numerous than the Egyptians, recalling how a small number of them had defeated large enemy forces without suffering any losses. Fearing that Israel's continued growth would pose a threat (especially if war broke out and they sided with Egypt's enemies), the counselors urged Pharaoh to devise a plan to gradually weaken and remove the Israelites before they became too strong to control.

This discussion directly connects to Exodus 1:10, where Pharaoh says, "Come, let us deal wisely with them..." reflecting a calculated effort to suppress Israel before they could rise further. The passage also draws a prophetic connection to Psalm 83:3–5, which speaks of nations conspiring against God's people with the intent to erase Israel's identity and existence. The passage says that they are confederate against God's people. This highlights a pattern of opposition in both history and future prophecy. When we examine the nations represented in this confederacy, a consistent picture emerges: Edomite/Roman powers and certain Arab nations—the same forces historically involved in the major slave trades, including the Transatlantic and Arab slave trades.

From the very beginning, there was a struggle between Esau and Jacob. Before they ever took their first breath, the brothers wrestled in the womb of Rebekah. What began as a physical struggle between twin brothers would echo through generations—becoming a spiritual conflict between two nations, two mindsets, and ultimately, two destinies. This struggle was not just about family drama. It was prophetic. It revealed a deeper battle: between flesh and spirit, pride and promise, rebellion and redemption. Genesis 25:27 tells us that Esau became a skillful hunter, a man of the field, while Jacob was a quiet man who dwelt in tents. Esau represents the flesh—driven by appetite, ruled by the moment. Jacob, though flawed, longed for the birthright and the blessing. Even today, this struggle exists inside each of us. The Apostle Paul recorded, *"For the desires of the flesh are against the Spirit, and the desires of the Spirit are against the flesh," (Galatians 5:17).*[155]

The descendants of Esau became Edom, a nation often in conflict with Israel. Edom stood opposed to God's people, even rejoicing when Jerusalem fell to the Babylonians. Because of this, the prophets declared judgment on Edom—most notably in the books of Jeremiah and Obadiah. God said He would make Edom small, despised, and exposed: *"Though thou exalt thyself as the eagle, and though thou set thy nest among the stars, thence will I bring thee down" (Obadiah 1:4, KJV).* And through Jeremiah: *"I will make thee small among the heathen, and despised among men. Thy terribleness hath deceived thee, and the pride of thine heart" (Jeremiah 49:15–16, KJV). Of* all the nations condemned in the prophetic writings, Edom receives the most intense and hostile judgment. Though the book of Obadiah is

[155] Galatians 5:17 (ESV).

the shortest in the Old Testament, it focuses solely on the judgment and destruction of Edom.

Image 14 - A picture of the Monastery in Petra, Jordan.

Image 15 - An Amphitheater-like structure in Petra.

The ancient city of Petra, once inhabited by the Edomites, features architectural structures that closely resemble Roman design, indicating significant cultural and political influence. Carved directly into rose-red rock cliffs, Petra's grand facades feature classical elements such as Corinthian columns, ornate pediments, and arched doorways—all hallmarks of Roman architecture. These similarities reflect Edom's assimilation into Roman culture.

Many believe that because Edom has been conquered throughout history, it no longer exists. However, the apocryphal book of 2 Esdras 6:9 says: *"For Esau is the end of the world, and Jacob is the beginning of it that followeth."*[156] This Scripture prophesies that Esau, also known as Edom, will rule for a set period—up to the end. After that, there will be a divine shift, and Jacob will rise as the beginning of the world to come. To truly identify Esau, it is important to understand that Edom refers not only to Esau's descendants but also to a broader identity. Edom represents a system of thought, a worldview rooted in dominance and rebellion. Historically, Edom is linked to Rome and its influence, which has spread and mingled with many nations. The Jewish Encyclopedia states, "The name 'Edom' is used by the Talmudists for the Roman empire, and they applied to Rome every passage of the Bible referring to Edom or to Esau." Edom is also described in Scripture as a continual adversary to the people of the Most-High, both physically and spiritually.

> *"I will lay thy cities waste, and thou shalt be desolate, and thou shalt know that I am the Lord. Because thou hast had a*

[156] 2 Esdras 6:9 (KJV). Also known as 4 Ezra, this apocalyptic text is included in some editions of the Apocrypha. It is preserved in the Latin Vulgate and the Slavonic Bible, among others.

perpetual hatred, and hast shed the blood of the children of Israel by the force of the sword in the time of their calamity" (Ezekiel 35:4–5, KJV).

Many events in history show the conflict between these two nations, Esau and Jacob. Here are some events, presented in no particular sequence:

- When Israel was journeying to the Promised Land, they requested to pass through Edomite territory peacefully, but Edom refused and came out against them with force.
- King Saul fought many enemies, including Edom, but was rejected by God for sparing King Agag and the best Amalekite animals—descendants of Esau through Eliphaz.
- Doeg, an Edomite and Saul's chief herdsman, betrayed God's priests at Nob, leading to the deaths of eighty-five priests.[157]
- King David established garrisons throughout Edom, and the Edomites became his subjects.
- The Amalekites regularly destroyed Israel's crops and livestock until Gideon, with only three hundred men, defeated the vast army that included them. King Solomon's downfall began when he married many foreign women (including Edomites), leading him into idolatry. God raised Hadad the Edomite as an adversary against him.
- During the reign of King Jehoram, Edom rebelled against Judah's rule and established independence.

---

[157] 1 Samuel 22:9–19 (KJV). Doeg the Edomite killed eighty-five priests at Nob on Saul's orders. David's response is recorded in Psalm 52.

- King Amaziah later achieved a military victory over Edom but committed the spiritual error of bringing back Edomite idols.
- When Babylon destroyed Jerusalem, Edom allied with them, killing Judeans and looting the city.
- Haman, a high-ranking official in the Persian Empire, was an Agagite—likely a descendant of Agag, king of the Amalekites, linking him to the seed of Esau.[158] Fueled by hatred when Mordecai refused to bow to him, Haman plotted to exterminate all the Hebrews in the Persian Empire. But Queen Esther exposed his plot, leading to his downfall.
- Herod, an Idumean (descendant of Edom), sought to kill Christ as a baby.[159]
- In John Chapter 8, the Pharisees claimed to be the offspring of Abraham, who had "never been enslaved to anyone."[160] This claim reflected their Edomite lineage rather than Jacobite lineage, for the descendants of Jacob had been enslaved in Egypt, Babylon, and Assyria. The Herodian dynasty stands as a striking example of Edomite oppression over the Jewish people. Herod the Great, an Edomite ruler, sought to legitimize his authority by marrying Mariamne, a descendant of the Maccabean (Hasmonean) line. Though he was

---

158 The Book of Esther. Haman is identified as an Agagite (Esther 3:1), linking him to Agag, king of the Amalekites (1 Samuel 15). The Amalekites descended from Amalek, grandson of Esau through Eliphaz (Genesis 36:12). The feast of Purim commemorates the deliverance of the Jews from Haman's plot.

159 Herod the Great (c. 73–4 BC) was an Idumean (Edomite) appointed King of Judea by the Roman Senate in 40 BC. He married Mariamne I, a Hasmonean (Maccabean) princess, to legitimize his rule among the Jewish populace. He later executed Mariamne, her mother Alexandra, and three of his own sons. See Peter Richardson, Herod: King of the Jews and Friend of the Romans (Columbia: University of South Carolina Press, 1996).

160 John 8:33 (ESV); cf. John 8:32 (KJV).

appointed King of Judea by Mark Antony, Herod governed through fear, deeply threatened by the enduring influence of the Maccabean bloodline among the Hebrew people. Consumed by suspicion and the fear of rebellion, he ordered the execution of Mariamne, her mother, and even three of his own sons. His reign was marked by a relentless effort to eliminate the Maccabean lineage—not merely because of any immediate political threat, but to suppress its legitimacy and influence among the people he ruled.

- The Romans destroyed the Second Temple and persecuted the seed of Jacob. The Romans persecuted early Christians fiercely, viewing them as a threat to both the social order and the imperial cult. Christians refused to worship the emperor or the Roman gods, which was seen as rebellious and unpatriotic. This refusal often led to accusations of atheism, sedition, and antisocial behavior. Emperors like Nero notoriously blamed Christians for disasters like the Great Fire of Rome and subjected them to brutal punishments, including imprisonment, torture, and public execution.[161] Despite this persecution, the Christian faith continued to grow, fueled by the courage and steadfastness of believers who faced suffering with unwavering devotion. The Roman persecution, though severe, ultimately failed to extinguish true Christianity and instead helped spread its message throughout the empire.

[161] Nero is widely recorded in ancient sources such as Tacitus (*Annals* 15.44) as having blamed Christians for the Great Fire of Rome and subjecting them to severe persecution, including imprisonment, torture, and public executions, marking one of the earliest state-sponsored persecutions of Christians in the Roman Empire.

- Yahshua identified one of His own disciples as a devil: "Have not I chosen you twelve, and one of you is a devil?" (John 6:70).[162] Judas, an Edomite, was the betrayer of Christ.
- When Yahshua entered the temple and saw the money changers, He drove them out, declaring, "My house shall be called a house of prayer, but you have made it a den of thieves."[163]

One significant thing about Edomite converts is that they've always had a financial background.[164] The temple, meant to be a sacred place of worship, had become a place of greed and exploitation, especially targeting poor pilgrims who came to offer sacrifices. By cleansing the temple, Yahshua was not only condemning corruption within religious leadership but also asserting His authority as the Messiah and zeal for His Father's house, fulfilling prophetic Scripture. This bold act marked a turning point, intensifying opposition from the religious leaders. These same money changers would create a system that is alive today. They had a foreign exchange system, and that system is alive and well all over the world.

For centuries, Esau's descendants have oppressed Jacob's descendants and many others. They have consistently lied, renamed many things, and disguised themselves through multiple identities to

---

[162] John 6:70 (KJV).

[163] In this passage, Christ cleanses the temple, rebuking those who had turned a sacred place of worship into a center of corruption and profit. Quoting Isaiah 56:7 and Jeremiah 7:11, He declared that the temple was meant to be "a house of prayer" rather than "a den of thieves," revealing God's displeasure with religious exploitation and the misuse of holy things. See the Gospel of Matthew 21:12–13.

[164] In the ancient world, Edom controlled what was called "The King's Highway," and they became crucial traders—taxing everyone that passed through their area. This made them wealthy.

hide their true origins and actions. Although they claim to be a "holy" nation, their actions reveal them as the opposite. This is a clear indicator of who they are. Edom is not just a people; it's a systematic way of thinking. Who they are is revealed in how they act towards humanity, especially towards Jacob's true seed in the Earth.

Following the fall of Jerusalem to the Babylonians, many in Judea believed that God had abandoned them. In their despair, they feared that Esau had taken their place as the chosen nation. In response, the prophets sought to correct this misconception. Their message was clear: despite the devastation, Judah remained God's chosen people. Through the Prophet Malachi, we hear God's sentiments:

> *"I have loved you, saith the LORD. Yet ye say, Wherein hast thou loved us? Was not Esau Jacob's brother? saith the LORD: yet I loved Jacob, and I hated Esau, and laid his mountains and his heritage waste for the dragons of the wilderness" (Malachi 1:2–3, KJV).*

We must know that the favor of the Most-High and the rising of the true descendants of the Hebrews of the Bible will stand as undeniable confirmation of God's Word. As we observe the world and the signs of the times, the moment we witness the Most-High lifting Jacob's descendants from oppression, we will know that prophecy is being fulfilled. In that hour, the downfall and desolation of Edom will be near. Take heart—though we have endured much hardship, our day is near. The hand of the Most-High will gather His people once more, and all will know that He has loved them.

> *"Behold, I will make them of the synagogue of Satan, which say they are Jews, and are not, but do lie; behold, I will make*

them to come and worship before thy feet, and to know that I have loved thee" (Revelation 3:9, KJV).

CHAPTER SIX

Exodus

The book of Exodus, as we understand it, tells the story of the enslavement of the children of Israel and how they were eventually delivered. However, at its core, it is a powerful demonstration of God's love for His chosen people. His love is revealed through miracles, deliverance, and divine blessings. A key principle throughout the story is that receiving these blessings requires obedience to God. Previously, we left off with the story of Zepho, the grandson of Esau, who led an alliance of armies against Egypt and the Israelites. In the heat of battle, the Egyptians, fearing the intensity of the fight, abandoned the Israelites. Despite being outnumbered, only 150 Israelite warriors fought and miraculously killed 2,000 enemy soldiers—and yet, not a single Israelite died. This victory was clearly attributed to God's presence with His people.

In the Book of Jasher, Chapter 64, after the battle, the Israelite men, still angry over the Egyptian betrayal, encountered some Egyptians along the road back to Egypt.[165] In their anger, they killed them for deserting them in battle, and others witnessed this act along the road. As a result, the Egyptians grew fearful that the Israelites, who were already multiplying, might rise and overtake Egypt. In response to

---

[165] *The Book of Jasher* records that after the conflict, certain Israelite men, still enraged by the Egyptians' previous mistreatment and betrayal, encountered Egyptians along the road and attacked them. This account appears in Jasher's expanded retelling of the Exodus traditions and is not found in the canonical biblical narrative. See *Book of Jasher*, Chapter 64.

this fear, they devised a plan to suppress and enslave the Israelites, which ultimately led to the period of bondage described in Exodus.

> *"And it came to pass after these things, that all the counsellors of Pharaoh, king of Egypt, and all the elders of Egypt assembled and came before the king and bowed down to the ground, and they sat before him. And the counsellors and elders of Egypt spoke unto the king, saying, Behold the people of the children of Israel is greater and mightier than we are, and thou knowest all the evil which they did to us in the road when we returned from battle. And thou hast also seen their strong power, for this power is unto them from their fathers, for but a few men stood up against a people numerous as the sand, and smote them at the edge of the sword, and of themselves not one has fallen, so that if they had been numerous they would then have utterly destroyed them. Now therefore give us counsel what to do with them, until we gradually destroy them from amongst us, lest they become too numerous for us in the land. For if the children of Israel should increase in the land, they will become an obstacle to us, and if any war should happen to take place, they with their great strength will join our enemy against us, and fight against us, destroy us from the land and go away from it" (Jasher 65:1–6).*

Exodus Chapter 1 tells us that this particular Pharaoh did not know the Israelites because Joseph and his brothers (the sons of Jacob) had died by this time. However, the Israelites were increasing in abundance, strength, and numbers. So, Pharaoh and his advisors devised a cunning plan to weaken and control the Israelites. You must know that whenever leadership is driven by fear instead of faith, oppression is around the corner. And fear left unchecked will always turn into force.

They issued a public call for volunteers from the Egyptians and the Israelites living in Goshen to help build the cities of Pithom and Rameses, promising daily wages for the work. At first, both Egyptians and Israelites worked together, and the Israelites received their pay. However, after a month, the Egyptians slowly and secretly withdrew from the labor, leaving the Israelites to continue the work alone. But the Israelites were still paid for a while to maintain the illusion of fairness. After about a year and four months, all Egyptian workers had fully withdrawn, only to return as taskmasters and overseers. They began to oppress the Israelites, forcing them to work without wages. Any Israelite who resisted or refused to work was beaten and forced back into labor. This exploitation became the foundation of Israel's enslavement, with the people working tirelessly on Egypt's construction projects for many years without pay.

Interestingly, the tribe of Levi was not part of this forced labor. From the beginning, they recognized the Egyptians' deceit and chose not to join the work. Because they had not been involved from the start, the Egyptians did not force them into slavery later on.[166] Ultimately, this account reveals how Pharaoh used gradual deceit to turn willing workers into slaves, setting the stage for Israel's oppression until God intervened to deliver them from Egypt.

---

[166] Book of Jasher, Chapter 65. The text notes that the Levites were not counted among the enslaved because they had not participated in the initial labor project and therefore were not later conscripted.

The Egyptians treated the Israelites with increasing severity, forcing them to work under harsh conditions. They subjected them to exhausting labor involving mortar, bricks, and various forms of fieldwork. Despite these efforts to break their spirit, the more the Egyptians afflicted the Israelites, the more they multiplied and grew in strength. This caused great distress among the Egyptians, who already feared being outnumbered and overpowered. Affliction was meant to break the Israelites, but it became the fertilizer for growth. Chains can't stop the promise. Whips can't silence the worship. Laws can't cancel destiny. The very pressure meant to crush purpose was used to press it forward.

The strategy behind Egypt's oppression was a plan of gradual destruction. As recorded in the Book of Jasher 65:5, the Egyptian leaders sought counsel on how to slowly eliminate the Israelites from among them, fearing their growing numbers. This same tactic of gradual destruction is seen throughout history, where systems have been used to suppress and weaken our communities—through abortion clinics, drug infiltration, slavery, segregation laws like Jim Crow, sinful natures, sexual immorality, dysfunction, broken homes, murder, poverty, and alcohol abuse; all aimed at keeping people oppressed and under control. Ultimately, the Egyptians feared that if the Israelites became too strong or numerous, they would rise up and destroy them or escape their control. This same fear, some argue, continues to manifest in modern systems designed to keep certain groups from gaining strength or independence.

The Hebrew historian Josephus tells us in *Antiquities of the Jews* that Balaam was originally in Africa with King Angeas during the time of Zepho, as discussed in the last chapter, "2 Nations," but was now a consultant to Pharaoh.[167] He prophesied that a child would soon be born to the Israelites who, if allowed to live, would grow up to overthrow Egypt's power and elevate the Israelites. This child was prophesied to be virtuous and remembered for generations. Fearing this, Pharaoh ordered that every Hebrew male child be thrown into the river and killed. He instructed Egyptian midwives (who served the Hebrews and were loyal to Pharaoh) to monitor Hebrew births and ensure that this command was carried out. Any family that tried to hide or save their sons would also be put to death.

This decree caused immense suffering among the Israelites. Parents not only lost their sons but were also forced to participate in their destruction, fearing for their own lives. The intent was not just to kill the children, but to slowly eliminate the Hebrew nation. As families were broken and hope faded, their grief deepened. This marked a dark and painful chapter for the Israelites, as they faced the systematic destruction of their people.

> *"And Pharaoh ordered his officers daily to go to Goshen to seek the babes of the children of Israel. And when they had sought and found one, they took it from its mother's bosom by force, and threw it into the river, but the female child they left with its mother; thus did the Egyptians do to the Israelites all the days" (Jasher 67:60–61).*

What is significant is that, according to Exodus Chapter 1, the midwives reported to Pharaoh that the Hebrew women were not like

---

[167] Josephus, *Antiquities of the Jews*, 2.9.2-3. Josephus records that an Egyptian scribe (identified in Jewish tradition as Balaam) prophesied to Pharaoh about the birth of a Hebrew child who would threaten Egypt's dominion. See William Whiston, trans. The Works of Josephus (Peabody, MA: Hendrickson, 1987).

the Egyptian women because they were vigorous. Before the midwives could reach them, they were already giving birth.[168] They thought forced labor and the rigorous sun would kill the Hebrews off or prohibit them from multiplying, when in fact, the Hebrews were a strong people. The melanin in their skin absorbed the sun's rays and made them healthy and strong.

Moses (born to Amram and Jochebed) was hidden in a basket and placed in the Nile River under the care of his sister Miriam. He was discovered by Pharaoh's daughter, who raised him as her own son—evidence that Hebrews and Egyptians shared similar physical features. As Moses matured and approached forty, he began to reject his royal identity and to show compassion for his fellow Hebrews. This compassion drove him to kill an Egyptian taskmaster who was beating a Hebrew slave. Fearing the consequences, Moses fled Egypt and settled in Midian near Mount Sinai, where he married Zipporah, the daughter of Jethro (also called Reuel), and lived for forty years.

In the Wilderness of Midian, Moses encounters the burning bush. God tells him that He's heard the cry of his people and wants him to go to Pharaoh and tell him to let his people go. This miraculous event was meant to capture Moses' attention so that God could give him instructions. Following this encounter, Moses began his journey back to Egypt to confront Pharaoh (believed to be Rameses II),[169] so that he could demonstrate God's power and lead the Hebrews out of

---

[168] Exodus 1:19 (KJV): "And the midwives said unto Pharaoh, Because the Hebrew women are not as the Egyptian women; for they are lively, and are delivered ere the midwives come in unto them."

[169] The identification of the Pharaoh of the Exodus remains debated among scholars. Ramesses II (c. 1279–1213 BC) is the most commonly cited candidate, though some scholars propose Amenhotep II or Thutmose III. See Kenneth A. Kitchen, On the Reliability of the Old Testament (Grand Rapids: Eerdmans, 2003).

Egyptian oppression, however, before his return, he gives the Most-High a distinct response to His request: *"And Moses said unto God, Who am I, that I should go unto Pharaoh, and that I should bring forth the children of Israel out of Egypt?" (Exodus 3:11).*[170]

Moses asks a pivotal question when he says, 'Who am I?' In that moment, he experiences an identity crisis and overlooks an essential truth: regardless of where he is now, his past carries the weight of royalty. The hand of God had been on his life from the very beginning. When he could have been killed as an infant, God intervened and spared him, allowing him to be raised by Pharaoh's daughter. He grew up as a prince in Egypt, enjoying privilege and education. But even before his time in the palace, he belonged to the tribe of Levi—a lineage set apart. Moses may have questioned his worth, but his story reveals a life shaped and guided by divine intention.

What is significant about Levi? This tribe was uniquely set apart for God's service. Unlike the other tribes of Israel, who each received a portion of land as their inheritance, the Levites were given something far greater—their inheritance was God Himself. Chosen by God to serve in a special capacity, the Levites took on priestly duties and were responsible for various functions within the temple or tabernacle. These included caring for the furnishings, leading in music, and guarding the sanctuary. They also served as mediators between God and the people, offering sacrifices, upholding holiness, and teaching the Law. Their role was spiritual rather than military or political, placing them at the heart of Israel's covenant relationship with God. As such, the Levites became a symbol of spiritual leadership,

[170] Exodus 3:11 (KJV).

representing dedicated service, spiritual authority, and a sense of set-apart holiness.

> *"And I, behold, I have taken the Levites from among the children of Israel instead of all the firstborn that openeth the matrix among the children of Israel: therefore the Levites shall be mine" (Numbers 3:12, KJV).*

Moses was from the tribe of Levi, so he was already of a priestly lineage; however, I do believe there's more that contributed to Moses being the right fit for the job. The Book of Jasher says Moses was a king in Ethiopia, the land of Cush.[171]

> *"In the fifty-fifth year of the reign of Pharaoh king of Egypt, that is in the hundred and fifty-seventh year of the Israelites going down into Egypt, reigned Moses in Cush. Moses was twenty-seven years old when he began to reign over Cush, and forty years did he reign. And the Lord granted Moses favor and grace in the eyes of all the children of Cush, and the children of Cush loved him exceedingly, so Moses was favored by the Lord and by men. And in the seventh day of his reign, all the children of Cush assembled and came before Moses and bowed down to him to the ground. And all the children spoke together in the presence of the king, saying, Give us counsel that we may see what is to be done to this city" (Jasher 73:1–5).*

---

[171] Book of Jasher 73:1–5. According to Jasher, Moses reigned as king over the land of Cush (Ethiopia) for forty years, beginning at age twenty-seven. See also Josephus, *Antiquities of the Jews*, 2.10, which records a tradition of Moses leading a military campaign into Ethiopia.

The Bible also calls Moses a king. This would refer to a later time after he brought Israel out of Egypt, but this is what the Scripture says: *"Moses commanded us a law, even the inheritance of the congregation of Jacob. And he was king in Jeshurun, when the heads of the people and the tribes of Israel were gathered together" (Deuteronomy 33:4–5).* Many scholars try to downplay this and present it as something more spiritual than it is. However, I do believe it was recorded this way because Moses was a king. And when he was king in Cush, which is another name for Ethiopia, that may be where he met his Ethiopian wife. Well, someone may say, "The land of Cush had nothing to do with the Midianites, and Zipporah was a Midianite."

According to Gert Muller in his book *The Ancient Black Hebrews: Abraham and His Family*, Midian, located in Arabia opposite southern Sinai, was inhabited by the Midianites—descendants of Abraham, also called Cushan. Moses married Zipporah, the daughter of the Midianite priest Jethro, who is referred to in Numbers 12:1 as a "Cushite," indicating that the Midianites were also known as Cushites.[172] If we allow Scripture to interpret, Habakkuk 3:7 indicates that Cushan and Midian were sometimes considered equivalent.[173] So, considering Moses was a prince in Egypt and possibly a king in the land of Cush, he already had experience as a leader. But when God

---

[172] Gert Muller, The Ancient Black Hebrews: Abraham and His Family (independently published, 2013). Muller argues that the Midianites were also known as Cushites, citing Numbers 12:1 and Habakkuk 3:7, a parallel between Cushan and Midian. See also the scholarly discussion in Steven L. McKenzie, "Moses' Cushite Wife," in Encyclopedia of the Bible and Its Reception, vol. 19 (Berlin: de Gruyter, 2021).

[173] Habakkuk 3:7 (KJV): "I saw the tents of Cushan in affliction: and the curtains of the land of Midian did tremble." The poetic parallelism between Cushan and Midian has led many scholars to conclude that these terms were sometimes used interchangeably.

confronts him in the wilderness by way of the burning bush, he says to the Most-High, "WHO AM I?" This is a true indicator that Moses was struggling with his identity, but what's amazing is that God still chose him. God was looking beyond Moses' internal conflict to reveal his external ability.

Do you know that common people could not freely approach or appear before the Pharaoh? Pharaohs in ancient Egypt were considered divine rulers, and their courts were highly structured, with a clear hierarchy. Access was restricted. Only those with specific roles or invitations were allowed into the royal presence. It's possible that when Moses returned, he was seen as a priest—but I believe the real reason Pharaoh gave Moses an ear was that Moses still carried a level of status. As I mentioned, according to the Book of Jasher and the Bible, He had a kingly status. The true struggle, however, was that the wilderness had challenged his identity. The wilderness always tests who you are at the core. Yahshua experienced this as well, and we'll explore it further in the chapter titled "The Attack on Identity". However, what's important to understand is that when God calls us, He's not focused on who we are in our current condition—He's focused on who He has called us to be. But to walk in that calling, we must first remember who we are.

Purpose doesn't begin with what you do; it begins with understanding who God created you to be. Life, pain, and people may try to make you forget your identity, but true purpose demands clarity. Like Moses, you may have run from your calling, but the moment you remember that you are chosen, loved, and called, everything changes. You can't fully step into your destiny while living under an identity imposed by fear or failure. True purpose starts when you stop running from who you are and start walking in who God says you are. Moses allowed his inadequacies to speak to disprove that he was the one for the task. Consider what the Scriptures reveal:

> *"And Moses answered and said, But, behold, they will not believe me, nor hearken unto my voice: for they will say, The Lord hath not appeared unto thee. And the Lord said unto him, What is that in thine hand? And he said, A rod. And he said, Cast it on the ground. And he cast it on the ground, and it became a serpent; and Moses fled from before it. And the Lord said unto Moses, Put forth thine hand, and take it by the tail. And he put forth his hand, and caught it, and it became a rod in his hand: That they may believe that the Lord God of their fathers, the God of Abraham, the God of Isaac, and the God of Jacob, hath appeared unto thee" (Exodus 4:1–5, KJV).*

As if that were not enough, Moses brought up yet another reason to argue that he was not the right person for the task:

> *"And Moses said unto the Lord, O my Lord, I am not eloquent, neither heretofore, nor since thou hast spoken unto thy servant: but I am slow of speech, and of a slow tongue. And the Lord said unto him, Who hath made man's mouth? or who maketh the dumb, or deaf, or the seeing, or the blind? have not I the Lord? Now therefore go, and I will be with thy mouth, and teach thee what thou shalt say" (Exodus 4:10–12, KJV).*

To walk in your true purpose, you have to get back into position. You can't fulfill a royal assignment while living in a distant land of distraction or discouragement. Like Moses, who had to leave the wilderness and return to Egypt, stepping into purpose requires returning to the place God called you to—whether that's spiritually, emotionally, or physically. Being out of position delays your progress and affects those connected to your destiny. But when you align yourself with God's will and take your rightful place, doors open, strength returns, and purpose is activated. Your position determines your power—so get back to where you belong. Seek the Most-High for divine alignment!

Likewise, to walk in your true purpose, you have to rise above your problems. Purpose doesn't mean there won't be problems, but it means refusing to let problems define you or derail you. Like Moses, who was weighed down by guilt, fear, and shame, many of us find ourselves stuck beneath the weight of our past. But you can't fulfill your future while being held hostage by yesterday. Rising above your problems means choosing healing over hiding, faith over fear, and destiny over defeat. God never called you to live under your circumstances—He called you to rise above them and walk in the power of your calling. Do you know who you are? You are royalty. Do you know who you are? You are chosen. Do you know who you are? You are more than where you have settled. It's time to stop running. It's time to stop hiding. It's time to silence the lies that the enemy has spoken. It's time to return to the position God called you to. You are the one that God chose, even when others overlooked you. You are the one who carries a purpose that's greater than your past. You are the one who can break the generational cycles. You are the one that God will use to shift the atmosphere. You are the one who was called for such a time as this. You are the one who still has a future, even after failure. You are the one who can bring light into dark places. You are the one who was born to lead, not follow the crowd. You are the one that hell tried to stop because heaven has a plan. Don't be stifled by an identity crisis; believe what God has said about you!

God uses Moses to show his mighty hand in Egypt. The Book of Jasher 80:1–48 recounts the plagues that the Most-High brought upon Egypt to compel Pharaoh to release the Children of Israel.[174] First, all the water in Egypt turned to blood at God's command, so that no one could drink it, and the Egyptians had no other source of water. However, it was sweet and fit for consumption by the Hebrews according to the *Antiquities of the Jews*.[175] Then frogs emerged from the waters and invaded the homes of the Egyptians—even their beds. These frogs spoiled the water supply again and left the country with slime, a smell, and an ultimate stink from the deaths of many frogs. The dust in the land became lice that affected humans, animals, and even Egypt's royalty, and they could not be cured with washes or ointments. Next, the Most-High sent a terrifying swarm of wild animals: fiery serpents, scorpions, toads, flies, hornets, fleas, mice, weasels, and many more. A sea creature called the Sulanuth even helped open rooftops and floors, allowing swarms to overrun homes.

Following that, a severe disease killed all Egyptian cattle, though none in Goshen (where the Israelites lived) died. The Egyptians' bodies became covered with boils that rotted their flesh. Then came a violent hailstorm mixed with fire, destroying trees, vegetation, and

---

[174] Book of Jasher 80:1–48. The ten plagues are also recorded in Exodus 7–12. Josephus provides additional details in *Antiquities of the Jews*, 2.14-15.
[175] Josephus, *Antiquities of the Jews*, 2.14.1. Josephus notes that the water that turned to blood was undrinkable for the Egyptians but remained sweet and drinkable for the Hebrews.

both man and beast. Locusts followed, devouring what the hail had left behind. The Egyptians tried to gather the locusts as food, but a wind blew them all away. Darkness then fell over Egypt for three days—a supernatural darkness so dense that no one could move from their place. When the darkness fell, anyone who was standing stayed frozen where they were; anyone sitting stayed sitting; those lying down stayed lying; and anyone walking just stopped and sat down right where they were. Finally, the Most-High gave the Israelites instructions for Passover. That same night, He struck down every firstborn in Egypt—both humans and animals. Even the images of the firstborn carved into Egyptian walls were destroyed, and the bones of long-dead firstborns were dragged from homes by dogs and thrown before the Egyptians. This final blow caused such horror that the Egyptians cried out with a loud voice.

This passage emphasizes not only God's power but also His justice. The plagues were not random—they were divine judgments on a nation that had brutally oppressed His people. However, the Book of Jasher notes that even some disobedient Israelites suffered during this time, reminding us that choosing the side of the Most-High is critical. God's justice is impartial, and His judgments are true. Also, the book reveals that Pharaoh himself suffered from leprosy and attempted to

heal himself using the blood of Hebrew children—further highlighting the cruelty of Egypt's leadership. This is still practiced today in pursuit of longevity. You must know that when Alexander the Great founded the city of Alexandria in Egypt, the Greeks were impressed by the intellect and achievements of the Egyptian people and wanted to explore further. So, the Great Library of Alexandria was founded. These people studied the history of the Egyptians and others, and adopted certain ways of life. It's no coincidence that people today are practicing the same practice the Pharaoh used to cure his leprosy.

In the end, Pharaoh ordered the Israelites to leave Egypt, and significantly, they left with great wealth. But as the Israelites departed, a familiar enemy reappeared—Edom. Edom's territory lay between Egypt and the Promised Land. To avoid the Philistine region, Israel had to pass through Edom, but the descendants of Esau opposed them. Edom assembled for battle, forcing Moses to reroute the people through the wilderness. This unexpected detour led to discouragement and complaints among the Israelites about Edom's refusal to let them pass.

The other issue they faced was the Amalekites. Remember, the Amalekites were a nomadic, hostile people descended from Esau, specifically through Esau's grandson, Amalek (Genesis 36:12). They are often portrayed in Scripture as relentless enemies of Israel.[176] When the Israelites came out of Egypt and were journeying through the wilderness, the Amalekites attacked them from behind. This attack is first recorded in Exodus 17:8–16.[177] As the Israelites were weary and vulnerable from travel, the Amalekites attacked the stragglers at the rear—primarily the weak, elderly, and tired. In response, Moses told Joshua to lead men into battle. Moses stood on a hill with his arms raised; as long as his hands were lifted, Israel

[176] Genesis 36:12 (KJV). Amalek was the son of Eliphaz (Esau's firstborn) by his concubine Timna.
[177] Exodus 17:8–16 (KJV). The Amalekites attacked the Israelites at Rephidim, targeting the weak and weary at the rear. See also Deuteronomy 25:17–18.

prevailed. When his hands dropped, Amalek began to win. Aaron and Hur helped Moses keep his hands raised until Israel defeated Amalek. Because of this cowardly and unprovoked attack, God declared that He would blot out the memory of Amalek from under heaven.[178] Israel was commanded to remember this injustice and to deal with Amalek when they were established in the Promised Land. Later in biblical history, Amalek is again seen attacking Israel during the time of the judges and even during the reigns of King Saul and King David—further fulfilling its role as a persistent enemy.

Because God showed Israel His mighty hand by striking Egypt, there should not have been any doubt as to God's favor on these people. Not only did he bring them out of bondage, but they left rich, and yet, as soon as they saw the Egyptians in pursuit, they became anxious and afraid.[179]

The Egyptians were always afraid that the Israelites would either one day destroy them or leave them. That's the fear that our enemies have today. They don't want us to increase in number or become strong. They fear that if we become strong, increase in number, or gain knowledge, we will destroy them. Yet, I do believe that this same instance will happen again. I believe there will be a time when God will gather his people again from the four corners of the Earth and bring them back to the land that was promised to them. He said it in His Word; however, I also believe that just like the Egyptians looked up and realized that they let the Israelites go, so will these other countries.

---

178 Deuteronomy 25:17–19 (NLT).
179 Exodus 14:5–9 (KJV).

In addition, they don't want us to leave because we are a gifted people. We build cities; we work hard (don't let them fool you, because we've always had a work ethic like no other); we excel in what we do, etc. So, they don't want us to leave, and the Egyptians didn't want the Israelites to leave. And one day they will look up and realize, "we've let the talent go, we let the slaves go, we let the entertainment go, we let the ones that built our countries go, we let our prize possession go, etc.," and this will trigger them to go after God's people again in which I believe that will be the fulfillment of the prophecy of Joel.

> *"For, behold, in those days, and in that time, when I shall bring again the captivity of Judah and Jerusalem, I will also gather all nations, and will bring them down into the valley of Jehoshaphat, and will plead with them there for my people and for my heritage Israel, whom they have scattered among the nations, and parted my land" (Joel 3:1–2, KJV).*

This is the event, I believe, that will initiate the Battle of Armageddon. As they pursue, an interruption will suddenly occur. As stated in Joel 3:16 (KJV), *"The LORD also shall roar out of Zion, and utter his voice from Jerusalem; and the heavens and the earth shall shake: but the LORD will be the hope of his people, and the strength of the children of Israel."* As Pharaoh and the Egyptians pursued the Israelites, the Israelites became overwhelmed with fear and cried out to the Most-High, blaming Moses for bringing them into the wilderness to die. In their panic, they preferred returning to bondage rather than facing uncertainty. But Moses responded by urging them not to fear, to stand still, and to trust God. He assured them that the Most-High would fight for them and that the enemy they saw would be defeated permanently if they would remain still and trust Him.[180]

God had already demonstrated his power with the plagues against Egypt, and after all of that, when the Israelites saw the Egyptians coming towards them in the distance, they were sore afraid. This was not a little fear—this was dread. Their lives flashed before their eyes. Let me encourage you—you may have believed you are facing the end. Like these Israelites, you may be dealing with something that has caused fear, but you have to know that if the enemy can introduce fear into your life, if he can get you afraid, then he can attack the strength of your faith, but your faith has to speak with a voice that's louder than your fears. Why? Fear will keep you from forward movement.

Because of the rerouting, the Israelites reached a stalemate. It was a large body of water in front, representing an overwhelming obstacle that could not be overcome without a miracle, and behind them was an advancing army, cutting them off from progress and ultimately bringing them back to their past. This is the enemy's tactic. He wants to bring you back to your past, but you have to be willing to declare that you are not going back. The future ahead of you may be uncertain, but you have to be assured that where God is taking you is a lot better than where you've come from!

---

180 Exodus 14:10–14 records Israel's fear as Pharaoh's army approached, revealing their struggle between faith and fear. Despite witnessing God's power in Egypt, they doubted His deliverance and preferred bondage over uncertainty. Moses' response, "Fear ye not, stand still, and see the salvation of the Lord," emphasizes a central biblical principle: that victory is not achieved through human effort alone, but through trusting in God's power to fight on behalf of His people (cf. 2 Chronicles 20:17; Isaiah 41:10).

The other thing we must deal with is discouragement. The enemy uses discouragement to drain our strength, destroy our confidence, hinder our faith, and keep us from moving forward.

> *"And they said unto Moses, Because there were no graves in Egypt, hast thou taken us away to die in the wilderness? wherefore hast thou dealt thus with us, to carry us forth out of Egypt? Is not this the word that we did tell thee in Egypt, saying, Let us alone, that we may serve the Egyptians? For it had been better for us to serve the Egyptians than that we should die in the wilderness" (Exodus 14:11–12, KJV).*

Discouragement is a common human experience. It can result from unresolved expectations, criticism, fatigue in the fight, spiritual attacks, etc. However, we must recognize that it's a weapon the enemy uses to slow momentum. Discouragement is real, but God has given us the ability to overcome it.

David said in Psalm 61:2, *"From the end of the earth will I cry unto thee, when my heart is overwhelmed: lead me to the rock* (the stable place) *that is higher* (that is on another level) *than I."*[181] The rock symbolizes a higher, unshakable place of stability—and our rock is the Most-High. When we feel overwhelmed or discouraged, we must anchor our hope in the Most-High. Though we may face battles, the good news is that we're not fighting alone. Those who belong to God not only have hope but also divine help. Consider the Israelites: they were trapped between the Red Sea (an unyielding barrier) and an approaching army. And this wasn't just any army; Pharaoh sent 600

---

[181] Psalm 61:2 (KJV).

of his best chariots after them. Those chariots were drawn by two horses, with one man driving and the other carrying weaponry. The horses were thoroughbreds known for their abilities, strength, and speed.

Josephus stated in the book, *The Antiquities of the Jews*, *"...with fifty thousand horsemen, and two hundred thousand footmen; all armed. They also seized on the passages by which they imagined the Hebrews might fly: shutting them up between inaccessible precipices, and the sea; for there was [on each side] a [ridge of] mountains, that terminated at the sea; which were impassable, by reason of their roughness, and obstructed their flight."*[182]

Even with all that was coming after the Israelites, God still made a way. My encouragement to you is this: never forget that God is fighting for you, even in the battles you cannot see. God is fighting for your freedom. Freedom is one of God's blessings. Yet so many people live in spiritual bondage (held back by fear, sin, addiction, and past wounds), but the good news is that God is not passive about your freedom—He is fighting for it! As stated in John 8:36, *"If the Son therefore shall make you free, ye shall be free indeed."*[183] And Paul declared, *"Stand fast therefore in the liberty wherewith Christ hath made us free, and be not entangled again with the yoke of bondage" (Galatians 5:1, KJV).*

He's also fighting on behalf of your faith. Faith in the life of a believer is constantly under attack—by doubt, trials, fear, and the enemy himself. But God is fighting for it! When you feel weak, when you

---

182 Josephus, *Antiquities of the Jews*, 2.15.3-4.
183 John 8:36 (KJV).

question, when you struggle—God is in the battle, and He is making sure that your faith remains strong. He's assuring you!

How do we respond to battles with faith? We need to pray and seek God's guidance, worship in the midst of battle, and speak and declare God's Word over our circumstances. When enemies rise against you, remember that God is your defender. Stay in faith and do not take matters into your own hands. Ephesians 6:16 in the ESV says, *"In all circumstances take up the shield of faith, with which you can extinguish all the flaming darts of the evil one."* And Proverbs 3:5 in the KJV says, *"Trust in the Lord with all thine heart; and lean not unto thine own understanding."*

Most importantly, God is fighting for your future. The Book of Jeremiah, the prophet, states, *"For I know the thoughts that I think toward you, saith the Lord, thoughts of peace, and not of evil, to give you an expected end" (Jeremiah 29:11, KJV). The* enemy does not want you to step into the future God has for you. He seeks to steal, kill, and destroy—but God has already secured your future.

> *"They have said, Come, and let us cut them off from being a nation; that the name of Israel may be no more in remembrance. For they have consulted together with one consent: they are confederate against thee: the tabernacles of Edom, and the Ishmaelites; of Moab, and the Hagarenes; Gebal, and Ammon, and Amalek; the Philistines with the inhabitants of Tyre; Assur also is joined with them" (Psalm 83:4–8, KJV).*

The Moabites were a people who wanted God's people to be cursed. The Ammonites were a ruthless people. The people of Gebal were mountain-dwellers who joined the fight against God's people. The Amalekites were the seed of Esau, who was also ruthless. The people of Tyre were a Phoenician people who often joined in celebrating the Israelite's demise. Assyrians eventually captured ten tribes of Israel and enslaved them.

All these enemies wanted to stop the future of God's people, but when God is fighting for your future, no enemy, no failure, no setback can stop what God has planned for you. When we feel overwhelmed, outnumbered, or powerless, God steps in. God does not ignore the attacks against His people. He actively protects and defends us. I love this Scripture in the Book of Psalms 34:17-18. It says in the ESV, *"When the righteous cry for help, the Lord hears and delivers them out of all their troubles. The Lord is near to the brokenhearted and saves the crushed in spirit."*

Whatever battle you are facing today, know this: God fights for you. Victory is not based on your strength but on His power. Stand firm, trust in the Most-High, and watch Him move on your behalf. You don't have to fear. You don't have to be discouraged because our God specializes in situations that seem as if you're at a disadvantage.

This is why we can't lose heart. This is why we can't faint in times of trouble. This is why we can't walk in defeat. This is why we can't give up at the first sign of adversity. Because with God we have the advantage. Remember what the Bible says in Romans 8:31: *"If God is for us, who can be against us?"*[184] So, as Moses said to the people, I say to you today:

---

[184] Romans 8:31 (ESV).

"Fear ye not, stand still, and see the salvation of the Lord, which he will shew to you today: for the Egyptians whom ye have seen today, ye shall see them again no more forever. The Lord shall fight for you, and ye shall hold your peace" (Exodus 14:13–14, KJV).

I truly believe there will be another Exodus. The signs are pointing to it. The real question is, will we be ready for it? Will we even have the desire to leave the house of bondage?

The truth is that prophecy is indeed being fulfilled. It was foretold that Esau would dwell in the blessings of Jacob and that Japhet would settle in the tents of Shem. Since they continue to occupy the land, it shows that God's true chosen people have not yet returned to their inheritance. But the time is coming, and God's word will surely be fulfilled.

"And I will bring them again into the land which I promised with an oath unto their fathers, Abraham, Isaac, and Jacob, and they shall be lords of it: and I will increase them, and they shall not be diminished. And I will make an everlasting covenant with them to be their God, and they shall be my people: and I will no more drive my people of Israel out of the land that I have given them" (Baruch 2:34–35, KJVA).[185]

These verses reveal a powerful promise from God—a restoration not only of land but of identity, purpose, and relationship. God declares that He will bring His people back into the land He swore to give their

---

[185] Baruch 2:34–35. The Book of Baruch is a deuterocanonical text attributed to Baruch ben Neriah, the scribe of the Prophet Jeremiah. It is included in the Catholic and Orthodox canons but not in the Protestant Bible.

forefathers. They will not return as strangers or wanderers but as rightful lords, blessed with increase and permanence.

> *"And I will bring you out from the people, and will gather you out of the countries wherein ye are scattered, with a mighty hand, and with a stretched out arm, and with fury poured out" (Ezekiel 20:34, KJV).*

Pharaoh thought his problem was the people, but his real problem was a promise. And here's the truth: Pharaoh didn't understand: You can chain bodies, but you cannot change promises. God has promised restoration, and when God restores His people to their land, it signifies the fulfillment of His word, the faithfulness of His covenant, and the beginning of lasting peace. A people once scattered will be gathered, strengthened, and rooted. And most importantly, God will dwell among them—not temporarily, but forever.

> *"For the Lord's portion is his people; Jacob is the lot of his inheritance" (Deuteronomy 32:9, KJV).*

CHAPTER SEVEN

Blessed/Cursed

"For it is time for judgment to begin at the household of God; and if it begins with us, what will be the outcome for those who do not obey the gospel of God?" (1 Peter 4:17, ESV).

During the Exodus, while Moses was on the mountaintop, God spoke with Moses for 40 days. He gave Moses the account of the history of the world from the beginning of creation to the present day and told him to record history so that generations may remember.[186] The Book of Jubilees, sometimes called the Lesser Genesis, is structured around the idea that history unfolds according to God's ordered plan, divided into jubilees, weeks, and days. This opening chapter sets the tone: God is omniscient, Israel is often unfaithful, but God's justice and covenantal presence remain consistent.

"And Moses went up into the mount of God, and the glory of the Lord abode on Mount Sinai, and a cloud overshadowed it six days. And He called to Moses on the seventh day out of the midst of the cloud, and the appearance of the glory of the Lord was like a flaming fire on the top of the mount. And Moses was on the Mount forty days and forty nights, and God taught him the earlier and the later history of the

---

[186] *Jubilees* 1:2–4 records that Moses was summoned to Mount Sinai, where the Most High instructed an angel to reveal to him the history of creation, the early generations of humanity, and future events concerning Israel. The passage presents *Jubilees* as a divine revelation given alongside the Law, emphasizing covenant obedience and warning of the consequences of rebellion.

> *division of all the days of the law and of the testimony" (Jubilees 1:2–4).*

The "forty days and forty nights" is symbolic of a complete period of divine instruction and testing (i.e., Noah's flood, Christ in the wilderness).[187] Unlike in Exodus, where the focus is often on the commandments or tabernacle, here the Book of Jubilees emphasizes God giving Moses a comprehensive chronological account, a sacred calendar of history, known as the "division of the days." This is central to the theology of Jubilees, which structures all of history around jubilees (49-year cycles) and emphasizes divine order and predetermined periods.

> *"And He said: 'Incline thine heart to every word which I shall speak to thee on this mount, and write them in a book in order that their generations may see how I have not forsaken them for all the evil which they have wrought in transgressing the covenant which I establish between Me and thee for their generations this day on Mount Sinai. And thus it will come to pass when all these things come upon them, that they will recognise that I am more righteous than they in all their judgments and in all their actions, and they will recognise that I have been truly with them" (Jubilees 1:5–6).*

---

[187] The phrase "forty days and forty nights" is frequently used in Scripture to signify a complete period of divine instruction, testing, or preparation, as seen in the account of Noah's Flood (Genesis 7:12) and in the temptation of Jesus Christ in the wilderness (Matthew 4:2), underscoring a divinely appointed season of trial leading to transformation.

The command to write is rooted in the idea that God's words are meant for future generations. Writing serves as a testimony—not merely of laws, but of God's faithfulness in the face of human failure. This introduces a key theme of the book: although Israel will repeatedly sin and break the covenant, God will not abandon them. The act of recording the divine words of the Most-High is both instructional and prophetic—future generations can know their people's history and look back to understand God's justice and mercy. God anticipates Israel's rebellion and apostasy, but He frames their future recognition as part of the divine plan. When punishment and exile come, it won't be arbitrary—it will be just. Yet these verses also contain an undercurrent of grace: even in judgment, God's presence remains constant.

The above verses in the Book of Jubilees also anticipate the cycles of sin, punishment, and restoration that will characterize Israel's history. It invites the reader (and the later community) to see their current sufferings not as abandonment, but as part of a larger, divinely ordained story. God's instruction to Moses is meant to create a sacred memory that grounds the people's identity in God's righteousness, even amid their failures. As God speaks to Moses, He doesn't merely relay laws; He reveals the moral structure of history itself. This opening section of Jubilees is not only a prologue to the rest of the book but a theological lens for understanding how a holy God engages a wayward people. There is both warning and reassurance: God knows Israel's future failures, but He has also made provision for their return. His faithfulness is not dependent on their perfection, but on His covenant. God, who is all-knowing and ever-present, already foresees the path the Israelites will choose, yet He still grants them the freedom to make their own decisions.

The Book of Jubilees 1:7–14 presents a prophetic vision in which God commands Moses to record Israel's future disobedience. Despite receiving abundance in the Promised Land, Israel will fall into idolatry, forsaking the covenant's commandments, sabbaths, festivals, and sanctuary. This spiritual unfaithfulness leads to social collapse, exile, and persecution of God's prophets. Yet hope remains: after judgment, a faithful remnant will return to God, emphasizing repentance, restoration, and God's enduring mercy—a pattern echoed throughout Scripture.

Life is full of choices. Some seem small and insignificant, like what to eat for breakfast, while others carry eternal weight, like choosing to follow Christ. The truth is that every choice we make brings us the results of that choice. Deuteronomy 30:19–20 shows us that God has set before us two paths (blessings and curses, life and death), and He calls us to choose life. Imagine two roads. One is paved and well-lit, leading to a flourishing garden; the other is dark and broken, leading to a dead end. Both roads are choices we face daily.[188]

Throughout our lives, we make hundreds of decisions each week. In fact, researchers believe we make thousands of choices as soon as we wake up. The issue we have is that, because we do this daily, making

---

188 Researchers estimate that the average person makes thousands of decisions each day, ranging from small subconscious choices to major intentional ones. Some studies suggest adults make tens of thousands of daily decisions, including habits, reactions, conversations, and behavioral responses, demonstrating how constant decision-making shapes daily life and personal direction. See Roy F. Baumeister and John Tierney, *Willpower: Rediscovering the Greatest Human Strength* (New York: Penguin Press, 2011).

choices can operate on autopilot or become second nature (without conscious effort). Psychologists suggest that most of our decisions are driven by the subconscious mind, meaning we often act out of habit without even realizing it. We don't always make choices with conscious thought. Yet isn't it fascinating that despite having free will and the power to choose, the moment a decision is made, the power shifts—suddenly, the decision begins to shape and take hold of you?

When you make a choice, you give it the power to shape your life. Out of God's deep love for us, He has given us the freedom to choose, and He desires that we would freely choose Him. He doesn't force our love or obedience—instead, He invites it. We aren't robots, and with that freedom comes responsibility. Every decision we make carries the power to shape our outcomes. Before making a choice, we must consider its impact. If I choose wisely, I empower that decision to bring forth good results. In the same way, choosing what is right activates the blessings or benefits that come from making the right decisions.

What makes choosing complex is the sheer number of options. It would be easy to love God if there weren't other things trying to take His place. It would be easy to give freely if it weren't for all the bills and other expenses that keep soaking up your money. It would be easy to walk upright if there weren't many other enticements trying to get you to sin. But having many options doesn't guarantee true satisfaction. Our lives are shaped by the choices we make, but sin often clouds our judgment. Instead of choosing the blessings God desires for us, we can end up making decisions that keep us in a state of spiritual bondage.

The Most-High was trying to take the Children of Israel to a better place, to their Promised Land, to their destiny, etc. However, every time they ran into difficulty, whether it was the threat of armies coming to wage war against them, or they ran out of food, or whatever else, they began to complain and say that it would have been better to have stayed in Egypt. In addition, they were trying to hold on to the culture and customs they had become familiar with before leaving Egypt. They just wanted to live their lives without the restraints of fasting, praying, worshiping, consecrating, following guidelines, obeying commandments, being preached to, etc. And many people are like this today—they can't rock with "so-called religion" because they say there are too many rules. But the truth is, many people can't serve the God of Abraham, Isaac, and Jacob because they still carry Egypt's residue on them.

See, residue shows up when the pressure hits. Look at the people's mindset in Exodus: *"And they said unto Moses, because there were no graves in Egypt, hast thou taken us away to die in the wilderness? wherefore hast thou dealt thus with us, to carry us forth out of Egypt?"*[189] Notice that these people are free, but obstacles have revealed what's still a struggle within. Egyptian residue also speaks loudly when faith is tested, when comfort is threatened, or when God doesn't move fast enough.

---

[189] Exodus 14:11 (KJV) captures Israel's immediate reaction of fear and sarcasm when faced with danger, as they question Moses' leadership and God's plan. Their statement reflects a crisis of faith, where past bondage suddenly seems preferable to present uncertainty. This moment illustrates how quickly fear can distort perspective, causing people to forget God's previous deliverance and doubt His ability to sustain them moving forward (cf. Numbers 14:1–4; Psalm 106:7–8).

These people said: *"Is not this the word that we did tell thee in Egypt, saying, Let us alone, that we may serve the Egyptians? For it had been better for us to serve the Egyptians, than that we should die in the wilderness" (Exodus 14:12, KJV).* That's the voice of residue talking. Because residue will make bondage seem better when freedom is uncomfortable. There's a sort of comfort that many of our people find in oppression. Because living with residue allows us to resist responsibility and accountability—that's why Israel kept asking for a leader like Egypt had, a system like Egypt had, and a king like the nations had.

Residue always seeks to return to external control rather than internal obedience. So, God brought the people out of bondage and into the wilderness. The purpose was to purify them and prepare them for the promise. You can't inherit the promise while still thinking like a slave. Egyptian residue can't cross over the Jordan, can't build the Tabernacle God wanted, and can't occupy the land God gave; this is why a whole generation had to die off. So, when the Most-High is dealing with you, please know that He is not just trying to save and deliver you; He's trying to dismantle the Egyptian system within you.

While Moses was away on the mountaintop, the Israelites grew impatient and created a golden calf to worship and sacrifice to. They indulged in wild celebrations, including dancing and public nudity. The calf symbolized the Egyptian god Apis, who was also associated with the Canaanite deities El and Baal. Worship of these false gods was deeply corrupt, often involving immoral rituals such as dancing, sacrifices, and sexual perversion.[190]

Throughout the book of Numbers, the Israelites repeatedly rebelled against God and His leaders. They complained about hardships, questioned God's provision, and challenged Moses' authority. Figures like Miriam and Aaron opposed him, while Korah and others led a major uprising. The people also quarreled over food and spoke against both God and Moses, revealing a continual spirit of discontent and distrust during their wilderness journey.

> *"The Lord said to Moses, 'I have seen this people, and behold, they are an obstinate people'" (Exodus 32:9, ESV).*
>
> *"Understand therefore, that the LORD thy God giveth thee not this good land to possess it for thy righteousness; for thou art a stiff-necked people" (Deuteronomy 9:6, KJV).*[191]
>
> *"And the LORD said unto me, Arise, get thee down quickly from hence; for thy people which thou hast brought forth out of Egypt have corrupted themselves; they are quickly turned aside out of the way which I commanded them; they have*

---

[190] The golden calf (Exodus 32) is widely understood as reflecting the Egyptian cult of Apis, the sacred bull deity, or Hathor, the cow goddess. and parallels representations of Canaanite deities such as Baal (and, in a broader context, El). See John Day, Yahweh and the Gods and Goddesses of Canaan (Sheffield: Sheffield Academic Press, 2000). The worship of these deities was often accompanied by morally corrupt practices—including ritual dancing, sacrifices, and sexual immorality—as reflected in biblical accounts (Exodus 32:6; Psalm 106:19–20; 1 Kings 14:23–24) and supported by historical and archaeological studies of ancient Near Eastern religion (cf. John H. Walton, *Ancient Near Eastern Thought and the Old Testament*; K. L. Noll, *Canaan and Israel in Antiquity*).

[191] Deuteronomy 9:6 (KJV). The Hebrew word for "stiff-necked" (qesheh-oref) literally means "hard of neck," a metaphor drawn from an ox that refuses to turn when the yoke is applied.

made them a molten image. Furthermore the LORD spake unto me, saying, I have seen this people, and, behold, it is a stiff-necked people" (Deuteronomy 9:12–13, KJV).

"Only the LORD had a delight in thy fathers to love them, and he chose their seed after them, even you above all people, as it is this day. Circumcise therefore the foreskin of your heart, and be no more stiff-necked" (Deuteronomy 10:15–16, KJV).

Deuteronomy 28:1–14 lays out the blessings God promises to Israel if they diligently obey His voice and keep His commandments. God assures them that obedience will exalt them above all nations and cause blessings to overtake every area of their lives. They will be blessed in the city and in the field, in their families, their crops, and their livestock. Their coming in and going out will be blessed, and their enemies will be defeated before them. The Most-High will bless their storehouses, their work, and their land, establishing them as His holy people and making them a testimony to the nations. They will experience abundance, rain in its season, prosperity in goods, and fruitfulness in every area. God will make them the head and not the tail, above and not beneath, as long as they remain faithful to His commands and refuse to follow other false gods.

As the children of Israel journeyed through the wilderness, their numbers and strength intimidated the surrounding nations. The Moabites, led by King Balak, were particularly fearful and alarmed by the multitude of Israelites who had come out of Egypt and now camped nearby. Seeing their threat as overwhelming, Balak conspired with the Midianite elders. He sent messengers to Balaam, a prophet from Pethor in Mesopotamia, known for his ability to bless and curse with power.[192] Balak's request was straightforward: he wanted Balaam to curse Israel so they could be weakened and defeated.

Though Balaam was a known diviner, he initially sought God's counsel and was told not to go with Balak's men or curse the Israelites because they were blessed. However, Balak persisted, sending more honorable officials and greater promises of wealth and honor. Balaam outwardly claimed he would only do what God allowed, but the reward tempted his heart. Despite God's initial warning, He eventually allowed Balaam to go—testing his motives and revealing what lay in Balaam's heart. Balaam's desire for status and wealth displeased God, so much so that as Balaam traveled, the angel of the Most-High confronted him on the road.

In a moment both miraculous and humbling, Balaam's donkey saw the angel standing in their path, sword drawn, and turned away three times to avoid danger. Balaam, blind to the divine presence, beat the donkey in frustration. Then, in a supernatural event, God opened the donkey's mouth, and it spoke. Finally, Balaam's eyes were opened, and he saw the angel, who rebuked him for his reckless and disobedient path. Balaam repented, and the angel instructed him to continue, but only to speak the exact words God gave him. Upon arriving, Balaam met Balak, who was eager for him to curse Israel. However, Balaam made it clear that he had no power to go beyond God's command. He was then taken to view the Israelites from various vantage points and delivered four prophetic parables

---

192 Numbers 22–24 (KJV). The narrative of Balak and Balaam is also recorded in Josephus, *Antiquities of the Jews*, 4.6.

(oracles), each reaffirming Israel's blessing and the futility of attempting to curse those whom God had blessed.

In the first oracle (Numbers 23:7–12), Balaam declared he could not curse what God had not cursed. He marveled at Israel's uniqueness as a people set apart and expressed a desire to share in their destiny. Frustrated, King Balak accused him of doing the opposite of what he had been hired for. The second oracle (Numbers 23:18–24) emphasized God's unchanging nature: "God is not a man that He should lie." Balaam proclaimed that Israel's blessing could not be reversed, for God had not seen iniquity in Jacob and was covering their sin.

In the third oracle (Numbers 24:1–9), Balaam abandoned attempts at divination as the Spirit of God came upon him. Observing Israel's orderly camp, he praised their beauty and strength, again referencing the "unicorn," and prophesied their future victories: "Blessed is he that blesses you, and cursed is he that curses you." In his final oracle, Balaam shifted to a messianic vision, foretelling a "Star out of Jacob" and a "Scepter out of Israel"—symbols of a ruler who would defeat Moab and the descendants of Sheth, ultimately fulfilled in King David and ultimately in the Messiah. He also predicted the downfall of Edom, Amalek (the first to attack Israel after the Exodus), and the captivity of the Kenites by Assyria, confirming God's justice over Israel's enemies.

Perhaps most remarkably, Balaam sees far into the future and prophesies an affliction that will come "by ships from Chittim."[193]

---

[193] Numbers 24:24 (KJV). The reference to "ships from Chittim" afflicting Asshur and Eber is widely interpreted as a prophecy of Greco-Roman conquest. The

These ships, coming from the Mediterranean regions (often identified with Cyprus or the Aegean islands), will bring oppression to Asshur and Eber; the latter being the ancestor of the Hebrews (before they were called Hebrews, they were known as the children of Eber). This passage hints at the Greek/Roman conquests, in which the Gentiles would subdue Arab nations and others, bringing enslavement and domination. Yet, Balaam concludes with a warning: even Chittim (the source of this oppression) will ultimately perish. As stated in Chapter 5, "2 Nations," Chittim, or Kittim, is the original name for the area of Rome, but it was later expanded to include Greece and Macedonia.

During their journey to the Promised Land, Israel was under the protection and covering of the Most-High, and they were blessed above every nation. Yet they easily forgot—or forsook—what God had done for them, allowed pagan culture to influence them, and remained a stiff-necked and rebellious people. Blessings in our lives represent God's favor, provision, and presence. Curses symbolize separation from Him and the consequence of sin. God's desire was never to curse His people, but to bless them so that they would be a standard among all nations. However, God is just, and in His justice, He allows man's free will to be the deciding factor in His judgment. When Israel decided to rebel against the commands of the Most-High, they cursed themselves because they didn't realize that they were a covenant people.

Septuagint renders Chittim as "Kittim," associated with Cyprus and, by extension, the western Mediterranean and Rome.

What is a covenant?[194] While the dictionary may define it as a simple agreement or legal contract, a covenant goes far deeper than that. Unlike contracts, which are typically business arrangements with time limits, a covenant is a sacred, spiritual agreement designed to last a lifetime. It carries a depth of commitment and relational weight that far exceeds a temporary deal. And how was this covenant established? It was sealed through the shedding of blood.

> *"And Moses took the blood, and sprinkled it on the people, and said, Behold the blood of the covenant, which the Lord hath made with you concerning all these words" (Exodus 24:8, KJV).*

A contract is a limited, temporary agreement that can be broken, whereas a covenant is a lasting, lifelong bond. Many people overlook the deeper meaning of Israel's story in the Bible—that God entered into a covenant with them —and Scripture reveals how that covenant unfolded, reflecting God's deep desire to be close to His people. However, they allowed distractions and disobedience to disrupt that relationship. Even today, God longs to be close to us, but we often let other things stand in the way of that intimate connection.

> *"And all the people saw the thunderings, and the lightnings, and the noise of the trumpet, and the mountain smoking: and when the people saw it, they removed, and stood afar off. And they said unto Moses, Speak thou with us, and we will*

---

194 The Hebrew word for covenant is berith (ברית), denoting a solemn, binding agreement between two parties. Unlike modern contracts, biblical covenants were ratified through the shedding of blood (see Genesis 15:9–18; Exodus 24:8). See O. Palmer Robertson, The Christ of the Covenants (Phillipsburg, NJ: P&R Publishing, 1980).

hear: but let not God speak with us, lest we die. And Moses said unto the people, Fear not: for God is come to prove you, and that his fear may be before your faces, that ye sin not. And the people stood afar off, and Moses drew near unto the thick darkness where God was" (Exodus 20:18–21, KJV).

God delivered His people from bondage to bring them into a place of intimacy with Him, a place where He could be near and have direct fellowship with them. But instead of embracing that closeness, they chose distance. Out of fear, they refused to hear God's voice for themselves and preferred that Moses speak on their behalf. They chose to stay at a distance rather than to know God on a deeper level. This same deception still affects us today. The enemy convinces us to fear God in the wrong way; not with reverence, but with shame, guilt, and feelings of inadequacy. We fear His power to transform us, and that fear builds a barrier between us and the closeness He desires.

Instead of truly engaging with God, we settle. We settle for learning about Him through social media, TV, or other people. We settle for surface-level worship, holding back our hearts even when God's presence is near. We let our minds stay cluttered, and our hearts stay distracted. And in doing so, we distance ourselves from the Most-High who longs to draw us close.

"This people draweth nigh unto me with their mouth, and honoureth me with their lips; but their heart is far from me" (Matthew 15:8, KJV).

If you choose to remain distant from God like the Children of Israel (if you continue to hold on to the barriers between you and Him), you'll end up wandering in the wilderness, never stepping into the fullness of the promise He has for you. Because the people chose distance over intimacy and would not allow the Most-High to govern, teach, nurture, and condition them for their future, God gave them laws and ordinances to govern their lives. These weren't just a few guidelines; there were over 600 commandments covering every area of life: Sabbath observance, circumcision, dietary restrictions, hygiene, social behavior, clothing, work, and more. The laws of the Covenant were given to shape the people's behavior, keeping them from forfeiting God's blessings, while ultimately pointing them toward something greater: the fulfillment found in the Gospel of Christ.

God's laws detailed offerings, sacrifices, festivals, purifications, and moral regulations to ensure holiness and devotion. Burnt, thank, and sin offerings involved animals, flour, oil, or wine, with specific rules for priests and the people. Festivals—Passover, Unleavened Bread, Pentecost, Tabernacles, and the Day of Atonement—added special sacrifices and rituals. Purity laws governed the Levites, priests, and all Israelites, covering diet, childbirth, illness, and moral conduct, with severe penalties for violations. Israel's camp structure and silver trumpets preserved order and direction within the nation. In response, the people pledged obedience: *"All that the Lord hath said will we do" (Exodus 24:7).*[195]

The Law given in the books of Deuteronomy and Leviticus contains many instructions governing worship, morality, and social conduct. For instance, it declares that any prophet who presumptuously speaks in God's name without being commanded, or who speaks in

---

195 Exodus 24:7 (KJV).

the name of other gods, is to be put to death (Deuteronomy 18:20). The people are forbidden to offer their children to Molech, a practice that would profane the name of God (Leviticus 18:21). They are also commanded not to eat meat containing blood and not to practice divination or fortune-telling (Leviticus 19:26). The law warns against slander and endangering a neighbor's life (Leviticus 19:16), and it prohibits cross-dressing, describing it as an abomination before God (Deuteronomy 22:5). Israelites are further instructed not to cut their bodies for the dead or tattoo themselves (Leviticus 19:28). They are reminded to bless the Most-High after eating and being satisfied in the good land He provides (Deuteronomy 8:10). In matters of labor and servitude, masters are commanded not to rule ruthlessly over others but to fear God (Leviticus 25:43), and when releasing a servant, they must not send him away empty-handed (Deuteronomy 15:13). Workers are to be paid their wages the same day so they will not cry out to God because of injustice (Deuteronomy 24:15). The law also regulates lending, permitting interest to be charged to foreigners but not to fellow Israelites (Deuteronomy 23:20). Finally, the law condemns a man lying with another man as with a woman, declaring it an abomination and prescribing the death penalty for such an act (Leviticus 20:13).

Here's what's important to understand about the Law: If we are under the Law, we stand guilty because no one has ever fully kept it. The Law wasn't given merely as a test to see who could follow it; rather, it was meant to reveal that salvation could never be attained through human effort alone. Its true purpose was to expose sin and reveal our need for something greater. Ultimately, the Law points us to perfection, and that perfection is found in Christ.

Galatians 3:10–13 teaches that anyone who relies on the Law is under a curse, for no one can keep it perfectly.[196] Justification comes through faith, not works, because Christ redeemed us by taking on the curse of the Law. While Judaizers in Galatia urged a return to the Old Covenant, the Gospel affirms salvation by grace through faith alone: *"For by grace you have been saved through faith. And this is not your own doing; it is the gift of God, not a result of works, so that no one may boast" (Ephesians 2:8–9, ESV)*. Also, according to Galatians, before faith in Christ was revealed, we were kept under the law, confined and waiting for the faith that was to come. In this way, the law acted like a teacher or guardian, bringing us to Christ so that we could be made right with God through faith. But now that faith has come, we are no longer under that guardian. Instead, through faith in the Messiah, we have become children of the Most-High.

> *"Wherefore the law was our schoolmaster to bring us unto Christ, that we might be justified by faith" (Galatians 3:24, KJV).*

It's important to note that the phrase *"to bring us"* is italicized in most Bible translations, indicating that it was not in the original Greek.[197] Translators added these words through interpretation, which, in this case, may be misleading. Without those added words, the verse reads, *"The law was our schoolmaster unto Christ,"* or *"until Christ came."*

---

[196] Epistle to the Galatians 3:10–13 teaches that all who rely on the works of the law are under a curse, for the law demands perfect obedience. Yet, Christ redeems believers from that curse by becoming a curse for them, as it is written, "Cursed is everyone who hangs on a tree," emphasizing that justification comes not by the law but through faith in Jesus Christ.

[197] Galatians 3:24–26 (KJV). The Greek word paidagogos ("schoolmaster" or "tutor") referred to a household slave who supervised a child's education and conduct until they reached maturity. It does not mean "teacher" in the modern sense but rather a guardian or custodian.

So, what does it mean that the law was our schoolmaster? In the original Greek, *"schoolmaster"* refers to a slave who acted as a tutor or guardian for children. This is further revealed in Galatians 4:1–2, which explains that although a child is an heir, they are no different from a servant while a minor. During this time, they are placed under tutors and governors until the time set by their father.

A governor or governess was essentially a private tutor, often employed in royal households to train and raise the children. These individuals taught the children everything, from how to sit and behave to how to manage schoolwork and cleanliness. Though the child was royal by birthright, they were still subject to the authority of the tutor or governor until they reached maturity. In the same way, the Law served as a schoolmaster for humanity. It was meant to teach, correct, even annoy—constantly reminding people of their sin and their need for something greater. Romans 3:20 reinforces this truth: *"Therefore by the deeds of the law there shall no flesh be justified in his sight: for by the law is the knowledge of sin."* The law was never meant to justify us; it was meant to reveal sin and make us aware of our need for salvation.

Even today, the laws of the land function in a similar way. They help shape moral behavior and establish a sense of right and wrong because humanity is naturally inclined toward sin. We need instruction, guidance, and correction—just as the Israelites did. When God called them to meet Him at the mountain, they were afraid and chose to keep their distance. They didn't understand God, and they preferred to deal with Moses instead. Like children in need of guidance, they required training. So, God gave them the Law—not as a final solution, but as a tutor to lead them until the appointed time.

Ultimately, the Law was only a shadow—a silhouette of something greater, more perfect, and complete. That fulfillment is found in Christ. As He said in the Gospel of John, Chapter 5, *"Search the Scriptures, for they testify of Me!"*[198]

Christ is the fulfiller of the Law and the provider of the New Covenant. Under the Law, we stood condemned, but through the New Covenant (through Christ), we are redeemed. He paid the ransom for us, delivering us from the kingdom of darkness and transferring us into the Kingdom of His Son. He saved us from the bondage of sin. We no longer have to perform endless rituals for atonement. Now, because of Christ, we can freely come to God, ask for forgiveness, and receive complete pardon for our sins.

As Galatians 3:13 says, *"Christ hath redeemed us from the curse of the law, being made a curse for us: for it is written, 'Cursed is every one that hangeth on a tree.'"*[199] This means that He took our place! We were the ones who deserved condemnation, yet He became our struggles, our issues, and our sins. He bore it all and died in my place, giving me the life that my own works could never earn. By the Law, we were guilty—condemned for our sins with no way to make ourselves righteous. The Law revealed our guilt but offered no solution. However, by the New Covenant, we are justified. Through faith and the grace of God, we receive justification that the Law could never provide.

---

[198] John 5:39 (KJV): "Search the scriptures; for in them ye think ye have eternal life: and they are they which testify of me."
[199] Galatians 3:13 (KJV).

As Galatians 2:16 explains, a person is not justified by the works of the Law but by faith in Christ. Likewise, Romans 6:14 reminds us that sin no longer has dominion over those who are not under the Law but under grace. This promise is for anyone who is in Christ. By the Law, we were sustained by rituals and ordinances, but by the New Covenant, we are sustained by faith. As Ephesians 2:8 in the ESV says, *"For by grace you have been saved through faith. And this is not your own doing; it is the gift of God."* It's not through our works, keeping the Law, or trying our hardest to be a good Christian that we are saved—it is through the work of Christ and our faith that salvation comes.

Our faith is what enables us to live a righteous life, remain committed to God, and be justified, for as the Bible declares, *"The just shall live by faith!" (Romans 1:17).*[200] When you embrace the New Covenant, you embrace something far more powerful. The Law was given to mankind on tablets of stone, but the fulfiller of the Law came from Heaven in human flesh. While the Law could only atone for sin, the fulfiller of the Law has the power to forgive sins completely.

I thank God that His plan for redemption was established before the foundation of the world; before I was born, before you were conceived, and before the world was framed. The Most-High had a plan of redemption and salvation, one greater than anything humanity could imagine. His plan surpassed the Law, the rituals of man, and the ordinances of man. It was the ultimate plan. Moses couldn't give life. The Law couldn't give life. The prophets couldn't give life. The kings couldn't give life. Good works couldn't give life.

---

[200] Romans 1:17 (KJV).

But through Christ, we have life and not just life, but life more abundantly. So, when you truly have faith in God, your actions will naturally align with that faith.

"For they being ignorant of God's righteousness, and going about to establish their own righteousness, have not submitted themselves unto the righteousness of God. For Christ is the end of the law for righteousness to every one that believeth" (Romans 10:3–4, KJV). The Old Covenant was conditional: if they obeyed, blessings would follow; if they disobeyed, curses would come. But God's ultimate goal wasn't just obedience; it was humility. He wanted them to realize they couldn't keep the Law on their own. He wanted them to recognize their need for Him, for a Savior. Yet in their pride, they believed they could handle it. Even today, some still believe they can earn righteousness through their own strength. But no matter how smart or disciplined we think we are, we still fall short. The Law was never meant to be fully kept; it was meant to reveal our need for grace.

Let's be honest:

- We can't keep ourselves from sin.
- We can't keep ourselves from making mistakes.
- We can't stop ourselves from making bad choices.
- We can't stop missing opportunities.
- We can't control our lust.
- We can't always resist temptation.

That's why **we need a Savior.** Not just to save us from the brokenness of the world, but to save us from ourselves. Because, as Scripture reminds us, *"there is no good thing that dwells in the flesh"*

(Romans 7:18).[201] The flesh not only refers to the human body, but also to the nature that exists apart from God. It represents the sinful ways, desires, and tendencies that are self-centered or rebellious. It also represents the inclinations that resist God's Will. Galatians Chapter 5 talks about this.

The difference between the Israelites and the other nations is that the other nations were not under the Law; only the Israelites were. Remember, the Gentiles are the seed of Japhet according to Genesis Chapter 10. In addition, remember that according to The Zondervan Compact Bible Dictionary, HAM was the youngest son of Noah and became the progenitor of the dark races; not the negroes, but the Egyptians, Ethiopians, Libyans, and Canaanites.[202] Therefore, the negroes are from the lineage of Shem (true Shemites), which is where the Hebrews come from through Eber. So, in other words, what the Zondervan Compact Bible Dictionary is really saying is that Israelites are negroes and, in addition, true sons of Shem.

God made a covenant specifically with Israel, promising blessings for obedience and curses for disobedience. Under this covenant, He instructed Moses to build the Tabernacle—a holy place where God would dwell among His people and where priests carried out sacrifices and worship. In Exodus 25:8, God says, *"Let them make Me a sanctuary, that I may dwell among them."* This reveals His desire to be near His people; not distant, but intimately present in their midst. Today, many argue that there's no longer a need for a physical

---

[201] Romans 7:18 (KJV): "For I know that in me (that is, in my flesh,) dwelleth no good thing: for to will is present with me; but how to perform that which is good I find not."

[202] Zondervan Compact Bible Dictionary, ed. T. Alton Bryant (Grand Rapids: Zondervan, 1967), s.v. "Ham."

building, and in part, that's true. Because of Christ, the presence of God now dwells within us. When we receive Yahshua and the Ruach HaKodesh (the Holy Spirit), we become living tabernacles—temples of God. The Bible says, *"What? know ye not that your body is the temple of the Holy Ghost which is in you, which ye have of God, and ye are not your own?" (1 Corinthians 6:19, KJV). But* even with that reality, there is still a purpose for the actual church.

There is something powerful about the corporate gathering. There's something powerful about coming together as one body, united in worship. While God moves individually, there's a unique anointing released when His people gather in unity. When voices rise together in praise, when hearts and minds align in worship, the atmosphere shifts and the supernatural begins to unfold. This is not a new concept. God introduced this structure during the time of Moses.

Yet the Tabernacle wasn't just a physical dwelling place—it was a visual representation of God's desired relationship with His people. Every part of it (the design, the materials, the layout, the rituals) was intentional. It was all meant to teach a greater truth: obedience births intimacy. Through obedience, God's people would express their love, honor, and trust in Him. That's why God gave Moses such detailed instructions—how to build the Tabernacle, what materials to use, how sacrifices were to be made, and which furnishings to include. It may seem like a long list of rules, but it was far more than that. It was a lesson in reverence, obedience, and holiness.

God was showing the Israelites something essential: He is holy, and we cannot approach Him casually. Worship must happen on God's terms, not our own. Some think faith is just about rules and consequences, but what they often miss is the deeper reality: we serve a holy God who calls us to walk by His Spirit, not by our flesh. His blueprint for living isn't meant to control us—it's meant to transform us. Scripture says, *"Be ye holy, for I am holy" (1 Peter 1:16).*[203] Yes, there are guidelines. Yes, there are standards not just in faith, but in every aspect of life. The real issue is not the presence of rules; it's the resistance of the flesh. Deep within human nature is a desire to be our own authority. That's why submitting to God's will is so vital. Without surrender, the kingdom of self will always try to reign.

The Tabernacle of Moses was called the sanctuary—a word rooted in *sanctus*, meaning holy.[204] It was meant to be a sacred, set-apart place. Sadly, in today's culture, many have lost respect for the sanctuary. Reverence has faded, and the sacredness of God's house is often overlooked. It seems that anything goes, and we've drifted from the awe and honor that once marked our worship spaces. But it's not too late to return. The call remains: to build lives and spaces that honor God's holiness. To gather not just as individuals, but as a unified body. To recognize that while God now dwells within us, He still moves powerfully among us—especially when we come together in faith, obedience, and reverence.

The Tabernacle symbolized Christ's human nature. Though it served a divine purpose, it was temporary; designed for a specific time and dispensation. Even as it continued to be used, it remained a powerful metaphor, reflecting the order and holiness of Christ. However, what

---

[203] 1 Peter 1:16 (KJV).

[204] The Tabernacle of Moses was referred to as the sanctuary, a term derived from the Latin *sanctus*, meaning "holy" or "set apart," highlighting that it was a sacred space designated for the dwelling presence of God among His people.

the Israelites didn't fully understand was that this temporary structure and its services could atone only for sin—they ultimately pointed forward to something greater. Hebrews 9:9–15 presents a contrast. The former tabernacle was great, but Christ's Kingdom, not made with hands, is a greater and more perfect tabernacle. The blood that was shed on the mercy seat has the power to forgive sin and cleanse from all unrighteousness.

Even though the Scriptures speak of about 5 main covenants, we can break the Bible down into two—the Old Covenant and the New Covenant (the Old Testament and the New Testament). The Old Covenant described God's relationship with His people (Israel), but the New Covenant described God's relationship with mankind. Under the Old Covenant, Israel was the focus of salvation. Under the New Covenant, the whole world was the focus of salvation. As many as would receive God and believe in His name, He gives the power to be called the Sons of God. The Old Covenant was merely a foreshadowing of the ONE to come. Everything pointed to the Messiah, who would fulfill God's promise.

The reason we must understand this is that we are in a time when many people are waking up to who we are as a people. They have realized that we are the true descendants of the biblical Hebrews. Because of this, many teach that we should keep the Old Covenant. They've taken the revelation of identity to extremes through philosophy and tactics, trying to lead people back to the Old Covenant. But the Old Covenant was not intended to be permanent. Hebrews Chapter 10 says that the Law was but a shadow of the good things to come.[205] Everything about the Old Covenant, the Tabernacle, the furnishings, and the rituals was to point us to the Messiah.

Through Him, we would no longer have to sacrifice animals to atone for sin; we can ask for forgiveness and receive it. Why? Because He paid the penalty for sin. He was the final atonement. Through Him, we would not need a priest to go to God on our behalf once a year. Why? Because He became the Great High Priest who is seated at the right hand of God, interceding for us. He removed barriers that separated us from His presence. He tore the veil and gave us access. Now we can come boldly to the throne of grace. Through Him, we no longer have to be afar off, but we can draw near to God with a true heart in full assurance of faith, with our hearts sprinkled clean from an evil conscience and our bodies washed with pure water. We don't need the blood of goats, bulls, sheep, etc. NO! His blood is enough!

The problem is that too many people are living under the Old Covenant rather than accepting the New Covenant that Christ has provided for us. Because of this, they are under the pressure of curses brought by the Old Covenant due to disobedience. My question to you, as you read this book, is: which covenant are you under?

The Book of Jeremiah 31:31–34 describes God's promise to establish a New Covenant with the house of Israel and the house of Judah.[206] Unlike the covenant made after the Exodus (which the people broke),

---

[205] Hebrews 10:1 (KJV).

[206] Book of Jeremiah 31:31–34 prophesies the establishment of a new covenant in which God would write His law upon the hearts of His people rather than on tablets of stone, promising an intimate relationship with Him, universal knowledge of the Lord among His people, and the complete forgiveness of sins.

this new covenant would place God's law in their hearts rather than in written commands alone. Under it, people would personally know God, and He would forgive their sins and remember their iniquity no more.

Embrace the new! Because in the new there is life, blessing, and promise. In the new, there is no condemnation—only restoration, grace, and redemption. This is why we must spread the Gospel of Christ: too many of our people are still living under the Old Covenant. Why does it apply to them? Because they are the true descendants of the Hebrews/Israelites, and the Hebrews/Israelites (not Israelis) are a Covenant people. So, this is why the media are always putting our faces on the news for crime; this is why entertainment uses us to promote the most debauchery they can; and this is why they shoot our people down in the streets with no thought. Our people are living under the Old Covenant because they haven't received the redemption of the New Covenant, and with the Old Covenant, there were curses (the curses of the Law).

Therefore, as descendants of the Israelites, we have two options in this life: to live under the Old Covenant or the New Covenant. Living under one brings condemnation and curses, while the other offers freedom. For those who are in Christ, there is no condemnation because the Law of the Spirit of life in Christ Jesus has set us free from the law of sin and death. This freedom is crucial to understand because it explains why oppression is so prevalent everywhere we go. We see it in many forms: financial struggles, police brutality, poverty, the difficulty of rising in life, and even the widespread drug trade in our neighborhoods. These are manifestations of the bondage and curses that come from living outside the freedom Christ offers.

If you are questioning this truth, let's look at some facts.

Systemic disparities affecting Black populations are evident both in the United States and across the globe, revealing patterns that extend beyond isolated incidents into deeply rooted structural inequalities. In the United States, Black Americans comprise approximately 13% of the population yet represent nearly 40% of the incarcerated, highlighting significant imbalances within the criminal justice system. These disparities are further reflected in sentencing outcomes, where Black defendants often receive longer sentences than white defendants for comparable offenses. Policing practices also demonstrate inequality, as Black individuals are disproportionately stopped, searched, arrested, and are significantly more likely to be killed during encounters with law enforcement.

Beyond the justice system, economic inequality remains a persistent issue. The median wealth of white families is nearly eight times that of Black families, accompanied by ongoing wage gaps in which Black workers earn substantially less on average. Unemployment rates for Black Americans consistently remain about twice as high as those for white Americans, reinforcing cycles of economic disadvantage. These inequities are compounded by disparities in education, where Black students are more likely to attend underfunded schools, face higher rates of disciplinary action, and have less access to advanced academic opportunities, all of which contribute to lower college completion rates.

Health outcomes also reflect systemic inequality, as Black Americans experience higher rates of chronic illnesses such as hypertension, diabetes, and heart disease, along with unequal access to quality healthcare. These disparities were made even more visible during the COVID-19 pandemic, which disproportionately impacted Black communities in infection rates, hospitalizations, and mortality. Housing inequality further exacerbates these challenges, as historic practices such as redlining and ongoing discrimination in lending and renting have resulted in lower homeownership rates and reduced opportunities for wealth accumulation. Additionally, barriers to full political participation remain, with voter suppression tactics and underrepresentation in political offices continuing to impact Black communities.

These patterns are not confined to the United States but are reflected globally. In Brazil, Black populations experience disproportionate levels of violence and economic disadvantage. In South Africa, despite the formal end of apartheid, economic inequality, unemployment, and land ownership disparities remain deeply entrenched. In the United Kingdom and France, Black populations face higher rates of police scrutiny, employment discrimination, and social inequality. Across Canada and Australia, systemic challenges persist in employment, policing, and social outcomes, particularly among Black and Indigenous populations. In Latin America, including Mexico and Panama, Afro-descendant communities often face marginalization in economic opportunity, healthcare access, and education. At the same time, in parts of Europe such as Germany and Spain, racial profiling and social exclusion remain ongoing concerns.

Even in regions where Black populations form the majority, such as Haiti, systemic challenges tied to poverty, political instability, and global inequities continue to shape outcomes, often compounded by issues of class and colorism. Across these varied national contexts, a consistent pattern emerges: racial disparities in justice, economics, health, and opportunity are not random but structural, reflecting historical legacies and present-day systems that continue to produce unequal outcomes for Black populations worldwide.

Do I believe our people are cursed? You can look at the history and get a clear picture of who the Israelites' true descendants are today. The Bible defines these people as being a people of the Covenant. There are blessings for obedience and curses for disobedience. Don't be deceived; other people groups know the covenant God made with His people and the consequences. Out of all people groups, we are the most oppressed. You can clearly look at the Black American in every country and see the same oppression. This ought to make you wonder why no other people group experiences this type of trauma, this type of disparity, this type of oppression, etc. I truly believe it is the result of our ancestors' disobedience to the Covenant and of our generation's disobedience.

Let's look at the example of the fig tree in the Gospel of Mark. In Mark 11:12–21, Christ, on the day after leaving Bethany, became hungry and approached a fig tree full of leaves, hoping to find fruit—but finding none, He declared that no one would ever eat from it again. He then entered Jerusalem and the temple, where He drove out those buying and selling, overturned the tables of the money changers, and rebuked them for turning God's house of prayer into a den of thieves, astonishing the crowds and alarming the religious leaders, who began plotting against Him. That evening, He left the city, and the next morning, the disciples saw that the fig tree had withered completely from the roots. Peter, in amazement, remarked that the tree Jesus had cursed was now dead.

Christ in this text is not operating as the Son of Man—in this moment, He is operating as God in the flesh, exercising His supremacy with an expectancy of fruit. For example, the fig tree didn't bear fruit because it wasn't in season, yet it should have recognized Christ's divinity and borne fruit simply because God was present in the flesh. Similarly, the people in the temple did not recognize Christ's divinity. They continued their transactions, so He overturned the tables and drove them out of the temple. The Nation of Israel as a whole failed to recognize His divinity, continuing in their transgressions, and as a result, they were cursed just like the fig tree.

Curses enter when people give in to sin, allowing Satan access to their lives. Sin opens doors for spiritual oppression, bringing emptiness, turmoil, and brokenness. Like putting money into pockets full of holes, life under a curse feels like an unseen losing battle. These curses can affect every area of life (mind, body, and finances) and cannot be broken by self-help or emotion, but through prayer, fasting, and surrender to the Most-High.

> *"The curse of the Lord is in the house of the wicked: but he blesseth the habitation of the just" (Proverbs 3:33, KJV).*

Obedience is the key to God's blessings because it aligns us with His will, opening the door for His favor and guidance in our lives. Scripture confirms that blessings follow obedience, as seen in Deuteronomy 28:1–2, where the Most-High promises blessings to those who diligently follow His commands. Obedience strengthens our faith, as trusting God's instructions leads to spiritual growth and deeper intimacy with Him. While disobedience brings consequences, repentance and a return to obedience restore us to God's blessings and grace.

Righteousness is the eligibility for God's blessings, positioning us for His favor by living in alignment with His Word. God honors those who walk in righteousness, as Psalm 5:12 states, *"For you bless the righteous, O Lord; you cover him with favor as with a shield."*[207] Righteousness is faith in action, showing our trust in God through obedience and integrity. Blessings flow from a heart devoted to righteousness, as Matthew 6:33 encourages, *"But seek first the kingdom of God and His righteousness, and all these things shall be added to you."*[208]

Our lives should bear fruit not by the world's standards, but by the expectation of the Most-High. A blessed thing becomes cursed when it fails to live up to these expectations. Many people live beneath God's expectations, and things become cursed when they go against His will. At that point, they become vulnerable to the curse's manifestation. However, Galatians 3:13 reminds us that *"Christ redeemed us from the curse of the law by becoming a curse for us."*[209] Just as the fig tree, Christ became what goes against the Law or God's expectation. On the cross, Christ bore the full weight of our sin and its curse so that we might live in God's blessing.

> *"For our sake he made him to be sin who knew no sin, so that in him we might become the righteousness of God" (2 Corinthians 5:21, ESV).*

---

[207] Psalm 5:12 (ESV).
[208] Matthew 6:33 (KJV).
[209] Galatians 3:13 (ESV).

Satan seeks to lead people away from God by causing them to forget Him, even though Scripture repeatedly calls us to remember our covenant with the Most-High. Israel forgot God through idolatry, adopting pagan practices, and rejecting the prophets, Christ, and the apostles, bringing judgment upon themselves (Psalm 9:17). Scripture teaches that life is a series of choices. In Deuteronomy 30:19–20, God sets before His people life and death, blessings and curses, urging them to choose life through obedience. God desires to bless His people, but disobedience brings the curses of the Law (Deuteronomy 28:15). Many remain under these curses when they reject the redemption offered through the New Covenant.

The real issue facing Black men and women is not the white man, lack of education, finances, or skin color—it is a covenant issue. Until this covenant issue is addressed, nothing will change, because a problem with the covenant is a problem with the God who established it. They can give public housing, food stamps, a Black President, remove Confederate statues, name streets after great Black men, change faces in government, and even offer reparations, but none of this will solve the problem. Because the real issue isn't political or social—it's spiritual. The root of the problem lies in the covenant and, ultimately, with the God of that covenant.

God's covenant and mercy remain, even when His people curse themselves. The Israelites' story serves as a warning, and we are called to learn from their mistakes—choosing faith over fear, obedience over rebellion, and blessing over cursing. When we align our words, thoughts, and actions with God's will, we open ourselves to His fullness, breaking the cycle of self-curse and walking boldly into the blessings He has prepared for us.

> *"But it shall come to pass, if thou wilt not hearken unto the voice of the Lord thy God, to observe to do all his commandments and his statutes which I command thee this day; that all these curses shall come upon thee, and overtake thee" (Deuteronomy 28:15, KJV).*

God has set before each of us blessings and curses, life and death. The choice is ours, but the good news is that through Christ our Messiah, we are empowered to choose life.

As you close this volume, remember that truth is not meant to simply inform you; it is meant to transform you. May what you have discovered lead you to walk boldly in the identity God has given you. The journey toward truth is far from over. Continue with me in *The Identity Crisis, Volume 2.*

List of Images

This is an index to all the images used in this book:

1. Wikimedia Commons contributors, "File:Greater one-horned rhino and baby at White Oak.jpg," *Wikimedia Commons,* https://commons.wikimedia.org/w/index.php?title=File:Greater_one-horned_rhino_and_baby_at_White_Oak.jpg&oldid=1210117890 (accessed June 5, 2026).
2. Image generated by Canva Ai from the prompt "Two-horned Rhinoceros."
3. Wikimedia Commons contributors, "File:Colorful shaded map of Middle East.jpg," *Wikimedia Commons,* https://commons.wikimedia.org/w/index.php?title=File:Colorful_shaded_map_of_Middle_East.jpg&oldid=865206415 (accessed June 5, 2026).
4. Wikimedia Commons contributors, "File:USS America (CV-66) in the Suez canal 1981.jpg," *Wikimedia Commons,* https://commons.wikimedia.org/w/index.php?title=File:USS_America_(CV-66)_in_the_Suez_canal_1981.jpg&oldid=1120007309 (accessed June 5, 2026).
5. Wikimedia Commons contributors, "File:Ben Gurion Canal compared to Suez Canal.webp," *Wikimedia Commons,* https://commons.wikimedia.org/w/index.php?title=File:Ben_Gurion_Canal_compared_to_Suez_Canal.webp&oldid=1148790384 (accessed June 5, 2026).
6. Image generated by Canva Ai from the prompt "Create a picture of jasper stones."
7. Image generated by Canva Ai from the prompt "Create a picture of sardius/carnelian stones."

8. Wikimedia Commons contributors, "File:Tomb painting from Gebelein, 1st Intermediate Period, 2118-1980 BCE; Egyptian Museum, Turin (1).jpg," *Wikimedia Commons,* https://commons.wikimedia.org/w/index.php?title=File:Tomb_painting_from_Gebelein,_1st_Intermediate_Period,_2118-1980_BCE;_Egyptian_Museum,_Turin_(1).jpg&oldid=919559366 (accessed June 5, 2026).

9. Wikimedia Commons contributors, "File:Abraham Isaac.jpg," *Wikimedia Commons,* https://commons.wikimedia.org/w/index.php?title=File:Abraham_Isaac.jpg&oldid=1200118418 (accessed June 5, 2026).

10. Wikimedia Commons contributors, "File:Hermonsnow.jpg," *Wikimedia Commons,* https://commons.wikimedia.org/w/index.php?title=File:Hermonsnow.jpg&oldid=1077289579 (accessed June 5, 2026).

11. Wikimedia Commons contributors, "File:Western Wall, Jerusalem, (16037897867).jpg," *Wikimedia Commons,* https://commons.wikimedia.org/w/index.php?title=File:Western_Wall,_Jerusalem,_(16037897867).jpg&oldid=1105082416 (accessed June 5, 2026).

12. Wikimedia Commons contributors, "File:Mountain jewish men.jpg," *Wikimedia Commons,* https://commons.wikimedia.org/w/index.php?title=File:Mountain_jewish_men.jpg&oldid=1093480662 (accessed June 5, 2026).

13. Wikimedia Commons contributors, "File:Caucasusian Jews with chokha.jpg," *Wikimedia Commons,* https://commons.wikimedia.org/w/index.php?title=File:Caucasusian_Jews_with_chokha.jpg&oldid=1106141818 (accessed June 5, 2026).

14. Wikimedia Commons contributors, "File:Petra Jordan BW 36.JPG," *Wikimedia Commons,* https://commons.wikimedia.org/w/index.php?title=File:Petra_Jordan_BW_36.JPG&oldid=1092195636 (accessed June 5, 2026).

15. Wikimedia Commons contributors, "File:Petra (20).jpg," *Wikimedia Commons,* https://commons.wikimedia.org/w/index.php?title=File:Petra_(20).jpg&oldid=1227271366 (accessed June 5, 2026).